SELL MORE.
FASTER.

RESULTS PRESS

Results Press
Unit 229
#180, 8601 Lincoln Blvd.
Los Angeles, California
90045

www.theresultspress.com

ISBN-13: 978-0-9988905-3-1

First Edition

Copyright © 2019 by **Kim Orlesky**

Dedication

To my sons, Marcus and Declan, who are growing every day and inspiring me to do the same.

To my husband, Shawn. None of this would have been possible without your encouragement, support and competitive nature.

Sell More.
Faster.

The Premium Solution Sales Process for
Getting the Premium Price

Kim Orlesky

Results Press

CONTENTS

Chapter One

It's All About Relationships

There is no secret to sales.

If you're hoping after reading this you're immediately going to know the secret sauce for selling premium services at premium prices, I'm sorry to disappoint you. There is no magic formula.

When we create higher value offerings to our clients, the sales process is longer, the relationships become more entrenched and the results become more fulfilling—or both parties.

Premium sales is all *relationship*.

Selling premium services is about how we connect on a more holistic scale with individuals and ultimately how we create more. Of everything.

Offering the very best services at luxury prices becomes less about what you say and do with your prospect and more about how we as human beings interact in natural conversation and an ongoing relationship. We ask more questions. We become genuinely interested in helping the other person. We believe amazing things can be accomplished when we work together.

Premium service providers look at every client interaction as a lifetime value. These are clients, partners and family members for life. And if the relationship matters, as it should, we take extra care in ensuring the relationship is always cared for.

We're all people. We like being treated one way and dislike being treated another. The closest thing to the secret of sales? Be a good person.

Be honest.
Deal with integrity.
Enjoy every moment.

Sales is fun. It truly is.

When you believe you will truly help people, are ready to share your impact with the world and love engaging and learning about other people, that's all sales is.

Chapter Two

Sell More. Faster.

In my first sales career, the end of the year was always the *big push*.

It was the last attempt to make our sales target and to achieve bonus status. If we were already at our revenue target for the year, commission rates were boosted. Every sale was worth more money. This is where the big dreams started to feel less like pipedreams and more like reality. Some reps would make more money in this one pay period than most people would make in one year. I was determined to be one of those reps.

The full month of December would be abuzz. I would hear chatter in the bullpen from several reps as they bragged about spending their bonuses and extra commissions on buying new vehicles, down payments for a condo or going on luxurious vacations.

For a select few of us who would make over 150% of the targeted plan, this also included a flight and four-night stay at a five-star resort with the senior executives of our company for the President's Club. Every year it was in some new, beautiful and exotic location. This year it was Maui.

For those who hadn't achieved their plan yet, this was the final push to make it past the goal line. It felt like the movie *Glengarry Glen Ross*—if you were at the top, there was nothing to worry about, but if you were at the bottom, the end of the year meant you had a lot of work ahead of you, which could also mean looking for a new job.

I was safe. I was better than safe. My year was already made. Now I was making a play not for another deal or two, but for whatever it took to become top rep of the year.

As the final days of the year came to a close, I was still making deals and smashing the gong in the middle of the bullpen, announcing another contract had been signed. I was on top of the world!

Beside me sat Keith. Keith struggled through every day. He fought tooth and nail to get every deal he could to date, and December weighed down on him heavier than anything else. Every day, Keith would come in and you could see the desperation on his face. He did the work. He worked hard. Some would even argue he worked harder than anyone else in the bullpen. But Keith couldn't close a deal if his life depended on it (and in some ways it did). Because as December came closer and closer to the end, it was his life at the company which was now in jeopardy.

My sales territory wasn't anything different than Keith's. We had the same number and mix of clients and prospects to go after. I wasn't a better salesperson than Keith. We went to Xerox sales school at the same time. At that time, he had two years of previous sales experience, whereas I'd started right out of university as my first job. So, all being equal, why was I sitting as #2 in the entire county and Keith was struggling to make ends meet?

It was *attitude*.

I continued to close more deals in December than any other month that year. In fact, I did almost three-months' worth of sales in that single month.

I booked meetings with clients to get to know them and their goals. I showed genuine interest in their business and showed them how I could help them save money—or many times how I could help them *make* more money by showing them how to sell a new product or service to their clients.

I was confident because I truly LOVED helping others. And when I left a meeting knowing, sale aside, I was helping another business and individual, my confidence grew.

Yes, I truly wanted more deals, but if I didn't get it in the month of December, I was also okay. My boss often told me, "Kim, we're still open in January. People will decide when the timing is right for them."

I wanted more deals, and I was working hard for every single one. Calling on former clients, and prospective new ones. Stopping in at locations with boxes of chocolates to introduce myself. I considered myself hungry, while Keith was desperate.

I was willing to work hard for a deal and be okay if the client said *yes* or *no*. Keith, on the other hand, needed *any* sale and tried to push for the *yes* as quickly as possible. He would put so much pressure on himself that he needed the *yes,* that if the client said *no,* it would crush him. The same way dogs can smell fear, clients can smell his desperation—and no one wants to say *yes* to a desperate salesperson.

Keith offered his prospects the deal of a lifetime. He would suggest there would never be another deal this good again. And if the client said *no*, he'd ask, "Well, why not?" and, "How come?"

He could argue his questions were focused on the client, but the truth was his mind was really focused on him.

He worried about how he was going to pay his bills and what he would do if he lost this job. He would put all his energy into every single client with whom he met, and despite giving it everything he had, they continually said *no*. Deflated, he'd go back to his car and try all over again until he was too exhausted to keep going. Day-by day, each time feeling more defeated and exhausted.

I think most of us have been there, or at least have known a Keith. Someone who tries with everything they've got and yet it's somehow not enough to get the sale. They walk around exhausted. They need every dollar that comes in and they will do anything for it. What's really happened is they forgot the reasons they are there to sell in the first place—it's to help someone else achieve their dreams—not them.

Zig Ziglar has a wonderful quote. *You can have everything you want in life when you help enough other people get what they want.*

Keith's dreams may have been fulfilled, but only after he connects deeply and helps others get what they want.

Keith's attitude needs to change, and then the sales will follow. Not the other way around.

So how did I know it was *attitude* and not some external factors?

Maybe Keith wasn't cut out for sales, which many people will say about themselves. Maybe despite what I said before, Keith's territory wasn't that great. Maybe it was completely tapped out of all potential sales, which is also something many people will say about their own client base, territories or service offerings. None of that was true.

There's an old sales joke about two shoe sales people who were sent to a remote island. Within a day of arriving, they each sent a message back to the head office.

Salesperson #1: *No opportunities here. No one wears shoes.*

Salesperson #2: *This island is a goldmine! No one wears shoes!*

Feeling he had to find a change, Keith left the company in the new year.

Within a couple of weeks, a new salesperson had taken over Keith's old territory. Shawna was brand new to sales and was one of the most positive people I'd ever met. She wasn't even finished her third month and she was trending to become one of the top salespeople in the company.

Shawna wasn't more skilled. The client base hadn't changed. Shawna was just genuinely keen. She was excited to help her clients. She came in every day, despite how bad it was the day before, ready to tackle the world and provide amazing value to everyone she interacted with.

More than anything, sales is an attitude. It's an attitude of giving, an attitude of being of service to others and always staying positive in the face of adversity.

Not every sale will go your way.

Not every person will understand the benefit of what your service will bring to them. That's okay.

Keep being positive. Keep believing in yourself. Keep sharing your gift with the world.

There is an art to sales. But sales is first and foremost a numbers game.

No matter how good you are, no matter how good your product or service is, you will never be able to find 100% of the people to whom you speak ready and able to buy in that moment.

Many conversations will take days, weeks, months and sometimes years before the prospect is fully ready. Keep being a better person every day. Don't take the rejection personally. One day that prospect will say *yes*, and when they do, they'll follow up by saying, "I wish we would have used you sooner."

The one thing which remains constant is making sales, building a business, creating your empire, whatever your dream holds, takes time and a lot of patience. If you tell yourself it's hard, everyone else can do it or you're not good enough, this game will take its toll on you.

If you want to be more successful in your business, value yours and others' time for what it is—*the* most valuable resource. Maximize it. Don't waste a single second of any day worrying about how you will pay your bills, where the next sale will come from or what you could have said or done differently in that last cold call, sales meeting or proposal. It's not worth it. Change it if you can and move on if you can't.

Being negative, anxious or worried doesn't solve anything. It doesn't serve anyone. Instead, ask yourself: *What could you be thinking about and doing instead to focus on creating abundance?*

We all have the same limited time in a day. For every second you are focused on something outside of your control, you rob yourself of time you could be focusing the same energy on creating something amazing.

Hours and days will pass you by. We all have the same 24 hours in a day. You can either choose to be obsessed with what you can't control or with what you can.

Chapter Three

Hand-Select Your Clients

Premium service providers set up their business differently than businesses that are selling transactional-type products or services. Premium service providers believe they don't need to sell to everyone—they just need to sell a few services.

This is more of the Jerry Maguire way of thinking. (And if you haven't watched this movie, sorry, major spoiler alerts…but really, you've had more than 20 years.)

See, Jerry was busy working as a sports agent. The company he worked for had hundreds of employees and likely tens-of-thousands of clients. Then one day, after aggressively competing for HOT rookie between him and someone he thought was his friend, he snapped. He came to the conclusion that it wasn't about going after more clients, but caring only about who was the top and forgetting about all the rest. It was about taking really good care of all the clients he as an agent had, even if that meant taking on fewer clients, generating less money (in the short term) and giving each client more personal attention.

In the end, because it's Hollywood, Jerry was someone able to make an amazing life only by having his single client bring him a wonderful lifestyle.

Now, being okay with just a single client is FAR too risky for anyone and I would never recommend that. With a single client, you are really set up, even if you are a contractor, as an employee. Your entire income is reliant on that one person.

However, when building the business of which you dream, you *do* need to be focused. We want to live off the Jerry Maguire motto, "Fewer clients. More personal attention." When we provide our clients an exceptional level of service, they will succeed, and so will we. They just need to pay for that higher level of service.

One of the first things I do with my students at **KO Sales U** is encourage them to get *really* clear that they need to create a list of 100 clients they will ultimately pursue.

Now you may be thinking, "Wow! One-hundred is a lot! I can't handle that many clients." The good news is—you won't. This is just the list of prospects. Not everyone on your prospect list will say *yes* when you call them (and yes, *actually* calling them). But it does help to keep the conversation focused and repeatable.

Reading that I'm only recommending a list of 100 prospects, you may have thought the opposite direction. "Wow! One-hundred is too little. There's no way I can create my business on so few prospects!" In which case, I challenge you. If selling 10 of your premium services to this list doesn't bring you to 100% (or relatively close) of your full-year revenue goal, you are selling your services too low. Or you're not strongly positioning yourself as the premium service provider.

Now I *wish* it only took 10 deals to make an entire year. Unfortunately for many businesses, that's not reality. But the idea is to shoot for the stars and land on the moon. Go for the big ones. Step into rejection. Settle for smaller deals when you have to. It will work out.

First and foremost, focus that energy. Be where your clients are. Reach out when you can't be in the same room. Go fishing in the stocked ponds.

Fish where there are Fish

I spend a lot of my time speaking at free events hosted by banks such as ATB when I'm in Alberta and other entrepreneurial organizations. (Yes, this is a very shameless plug for ATB. Most of my business wouldn't be where it is today without this relationship.). Oftentimes, my ideal clients are brand new to entrepreneurship and don't know where to turn for resources. The free talks I give provide many new business owners with the first concrete advice they need to create a sales process, and why having a process is SO important.

I love sharing my knowledge. Hence, one of the reasons I decided to write this book. I love helping people even more, which is why I will typically host free sales-strategy sessions after one of my events. I would also love to help you, too! Please reach out to me as you're going through this book, even if it's to tell me you're reading this book and are ready to take serious action on creating a sales strategy for yourself or your team. I'm here to help you navigate this information and turn that education into application. Email me directly at *Kim@KOAdvantage.com*.

I may speak at plenty of free events, but rarely do I attend free events to network. I find many people attending free networking events are there to search for likeminded individuals, and sometimes these events can turn into a pitch-fest where everyone starts walking around and plugging their product or service without taking a moment to get to know the person to whom they are speaking.

I'm not saying all events are like that, but a vast majority of them are.

I do attend paid networking events. Even the events we host will be anywhere from a $5 donation to charity to a $30 lunch and learn, with lunch included. Setting a price creates a slight barrier-to-entry for those who are serious about being in a quality room, and those who want to push business cards like they are handing out entertainment cards on the Vegas strip. And like the difference in a room from a "no-line free cover" to a hefty entry fee, the overall quality of the room increases, as well. By knowing you have to pay even just a little allows you and others to associate a certain amount of value to the event. Everyone is far more likely to commit to showing up.

On the events you decide either to host or attend, first get clear on who you want as an ideal client. What questions do they have? About what are they concerned (besides your product or service)? Where are they going to source that information?

By tailoring your message and reading the message of others, you will be able to go to where your ideal clients are.

There's a saying: *Fish where there are fish.* You would never go to a sparse pond hoping to catch a record-breaking fish. Nor would you go to a freshwater lake and try to fish for a fish which lives in the ocean.

Get clarity on who your ideal client is and make sure you are setting yourself up for success to meet them quickly.

To take time to understand who your ideal client is, we ask ourselves questions such as: *Where would we find this client? What would they be doing?*

A Dance School for Nurses

I once had a woman connect with me and ask if I would be willing to share some of my sales knowledge for her online business community. I was honored, and together we hosted an amazing sales conversation. When the session finished, one of the viewers reach out to me. She said the advice I'd given was great for a company that was looking for other business clients, but what about her? She owned a dance school in South Carolina. Her biggest struggle was to get more people signed up for monthly memberships.

I asked her, "What clients do you ideally like to work with?"

She told me she had a wide variety of people, but the ones who typically stayed as lifelong members were the nurses.

Many of the nurses she encountered had dreamed as little girls about becoming professional dancers. They'd danced two or three days a week when they were in school, but as life took over, it also took over the dream of becoming a professional dancer.

And that's why they loved her school. They felt young again. It was a great physical activity, and the movement of dance melted the stress away. As a business owner, this woman could feel the energy of the camaraderie build on the dance floor with these women who wore their superhero nurse scrubs by day and moved freely at night.

"That's it!" I explained to this woman. "Don't try to overcomplicate the solution to your problem. If you want more nurses, go get them!"

This confused the woman a bit.

"But how?" she questioned back.

"Print off some flyers and stop into every hospital, doctor's office, dentist's office and clinic in a six-mile range. Tell the receptionist what you just told me. You have a dance school and many of your members are nurses who as children dreamed to become professional dancers. Now, as adults, it's a great way to connect to that love, while at the same time melting away the stress of the day."

I told her if she stopped at three clinics every day for a month, her membership would be completely full by the end of the month.

Sure enough, it only took three weeks for every one of her classes to be booked that semester.

Understand Your Value before You Communicate it to Others

When we're in a sales cycle, we sometimes forget we should be in the power position. Starting from the days of the saying, "The Customer is Always Right," we began to put the client in the power position. And that is true for some things.

Our clients are special. They deserve to be treated as such. But somewhere along the line we forgot we also are special.

We forgot that our products and services *shouldn't* be offered to everyone. As premium service providers, we deal only with those individuals who appreciate and graciously welcome our presence.

Do you think the high-end car dealerships try to push every person they meet into being interested in their product? Of course not. If they did, they would find themselves far too busy with the individuals who will never buy nor truly appreciate their product, and in turn, those who are their ideal client would find themselves turned off by the lack of personal attention and the opportunity to feel exclusive.

Hosting a Party for Your Clients

Imagine you are hosting a high-end dinner party. You have limited resources for your party—only a select number of seats at the table, funds to spend on the event and time to dedicate to the guests who are in attendance. If you decide to invite everyone you've ever met, you may throw out a Facebook invite blast and end up with one of two different outcomes:

Either far too many people would show up and there wouldn't be enough chairs for everyone to feel comfortable. The quality of food offered would be lower as you opted for frozen appetizers over a plated dinner. Each person would only receive a small amount of your time, sometimes nothing more than a brief greeting. Guests (if you can call them that) would feel they were not fully-connecting with you personally. And yes, they might have a good time, but was that good time created by your personal involvement with them or with the general environment you'd created?

In a second scenario, you may only have a few people attend. The individuals who were craving your personal attention would likely not come because they didn't want to get lost in the crowd of people. You bought far too much food for the number of attendees, and although each person might receive their fill on the lower-valued offerings, you'd still diluted the entire experience. You gave the people their fill of low-priced beer instead of high-end champagne.

I had a friend who would do this for every invite she extended. She'd call and ask me and my husband to join her and her husband for dinner. But when we arrived, there were always more than 20 other people there. I loved spending time with her and looked forward to going over to her house for what I thought would be quality time as two couples. But when I arrived, I never had the opportunity to really get into a deep conversation. She was so busy entertaining everyone else in the room that I began to feel left out. Eventually, I learned her invites were never exclusive, and if I wanted to spend time with her, it would have to be on my terms, not by her invitation.

Now, as the party host, imagine instead you decide to invite those who love and appreciate what you have to offer.

You've extended your invitation to those you know will attend and appreciate the company you provide them. Perhaps this is only one other person, or maybe it's a handful of people. Regardless, each person at the table feels special. You've provided well-thought-out extra details such as place-settings with their names, a personal greeting when they arrive and extra time to have an engaging conversation with each person. The meal you provide is a high-quality spread with each dish selected specifically to accompany the subsequent courses. Your beverage choice is a high-end wine made to complement the flavors of each dish. And at the end of the night, you thank each person personally as they walk out the door for gracing you with their presence and conversation.

Which of those parties would you rather attend? Which one would you rather throw?

There's nothing wrong if you say you want to host the first party. I've attended my fair share throughout my lifetime. I know what to expect, and if that's the experience I'm looking for, I'm happy to put myself in that position. However, I also know when I attend a massive shaker, I am fully aware I will need to take care of myself, because the hostess has a lot of other people to greet and connect with while I'm there.

If you chose the higher-end dinner party as the one you would rather host, then ask yourself: Are you creating this high-end experience when your prospects engage with your product or service?

No matter what, you can't have both. You can't try to create plated dinners with table settings and then invite 100 people. The first few people to arrive will love it, but as more and more people show up, it ruins the entire experience for everyone.

The Value Triangle

The value triangle is a simple economics model for determining where your product, service and quality fit in.

In the value triangle you can have the best price, the best service, or the best quality of product. You can choose any two, but you can't have all three. If you try for all three, something will give, and it will be the market that decides. Usually, the market chooses the best price, which means either your quality or service must suffer.

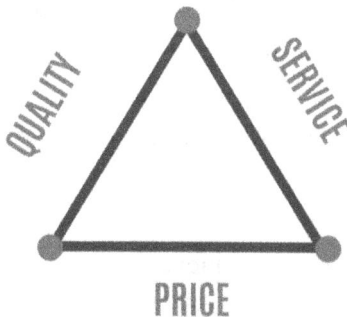

QUALITY   SERVICE

PRICE

An Example from Retailer Michael Kors

Throughout the late 90s and early 2000s, many premium and luxury retailers began to open specialty and boutique locations for their products. By 2017, as online shopping reached its peak, consumer spending in retail locations started to decrease and the competitive environment online became more heated. Plenty of retailers filed for bankruptcy protection.

Luxury brands such as Michael Kors typically served their clients with boutique stores. They created an experience for their product. Limited selection. Plenty of staff happy to walk with you throughout the store and chat with you about each product you looked at, held and tried on.

But as the Michael Kors name became more recognized, they decided to serve a larger selection of clients. They allowed discount retailers to sell their product at more locations across the country. They offered their high-end brand name at a reduced price. Suddenly, individuals who'd been interested in the premium product at the premium price were frustrated. Why would they spend two or three times the amount for the same product as everyone else? Yes, it may not have been the exact same quality item, but the challenge no longer became about the specific product—it was about the overall offering.

Consumers visited boutique locations less often. The Michael Kors name became diluted. It was no longer the high-end dinner party people wanted to attend—it was turning into the low-end shaker. And if an individual wanted to own a Michael Kors purse, did it matter if it came from a discount retailer or the boutique location? For most people, it didn't.

Michael Kors tried to be a bit of everything to everyone. They had to make a decision. They were offering a better-priced product at more locations, serving more people, while subsequently offering higher service to shop for their products for the premium price.

Michael Kors tried to play in two different fields at the same time, and since they couldn't make a decision, consumers made the decision for them. They chose to purchase their products at the better price, whether that meant at the discount retailers, or only if the products were reduced in price at the boutique locations.

Over time, Michael Kors had to make the difficult decision of closing several boutique locations. No one wanted the premium service at the premium price. They were okay having the premium quality at a mid-level price.

Where Do You Fit into the Value Triangle?

Where do you see your product or service-based product fitting into the value triangle? You can choose between the best price, best service, or best quality. You can choose any two, but you can't choose all three. Which two do you choose? And on which will you then not compromise? For example, if you want the best service and the best quality, you will not negotiate on price.

But remember, if you decide you want to have the best-priced product, know your limitations. After all, when the creator of *7-Minute Abs* came out he thought no one would beat him until someone released *6-Minute Abs*.

The last place you want to position yourself is in a race for the bottom.

Chapter Four

Revenue is a Lagging Indicator

When we set our goals for ourselves and our company, usually one of the first goals, and the most easily quantifiable, is a revenue target.

But as important as revenue is to achieve, it's not the area on which we should focus. Revenue is the result of the work we put in to our business every single day. That makes revenue the lagging indicator of the other tasks we need to measure in our business.

When we reverse-engineer the revenue goal to break down the tasks we need to perform in order to achieve the revenue goal, we end up calculating the number of prospects, the number of meetings and the number of proposals which need to be accomplished on a monthly or weekly basis.

Personally, I love breaking all this down to a weekly goal.

A week is easy to manage. It's also helpful to be sitting at your computer on Friday and know if you have enough meetings, proposals and dedicated time for prospecting booked in the week ahead to hit your goals. And if there isn't, now's the time to get cracking.

So how many calls, meetings and proposals do you need every week?

Take the revenue you want to make in a year (Annual Revenue), divide it by the Average Client Value and you'll get the number of clients you need for that year. Divide this further by 52 weeks to get a weekly target number of clients. (Less, if you like to take vacations. Personally, I use 44, because I like to have eight weeks of vacation a year.)

Annual Revenue / Average Client \$ = # of Clients per Year

# of Clients / 50 Work Weeks per Year = # of Clients per Week

---

This is the starting point. Unless you are absolutely amazing in your sales and are able to create a client out of every person with whom you interact (and if you are, please do contact me, because I want to know your secret to success), this is just the beginning of the formula.

The next step is to figure out how many people with whom we need to interact to get to the right number of clients. This is called the *closing ratio*.

Closing ratios are one of those funny calculations because it can mean different things to different companies. Some companies will calculate their close ratio based on prospects who are at certain points in the sales cycle. Often this is based on those who make it to lead qualification. Some companies and individuals go deeper into their calculation by measuring when they met their most recent close and how many people they spoke to in order to get to the close, but this could require keeping months of detailed data.

Each industry and primary sales methodology may have a different close ratio. For instance, a person who walks into a Starbucks is more than 90% likely to become a customer. If you are trying to create an entirely online business, you will have closer to a 2% close ratio for the number of people who visit your website who actually convert into a paying client. But if you are determining your close ratio for the very first time, instead of over-complicating the process, it's a good idea just to get started and then adjust from there.

If you know your closing ratio, great! Skip the next section. If you need to calculate it for the first time (or recalculate it as your goals change and Average Client Value increases), I prefer using a simple method. It may not be completely accurate, but it's a good starting point. As you start selling and seeing how your actual numbers of meetings and average client deal sizes affect your goal results, make slight adjustments.

Remember, you are measuring the tasks to get to the goal.

Let's now determine the total number of prospects with whom you need to be engaged weekly.

Calculating the Number of Weekly Activities

Sales 101 tells us that for every 10 prospects we meet, one will agree to a meeting and eventually become our client.

We don't rely on every person we meet to become a client. That puts too much pressure on the relationship. Timing, budget, people and needs can all change at various times throughout the sales process. Let's instead make sure we have more meetings booked with prospects than are needed in order to make our revenue target.

I recommend having four times as many meetings booked as the number of sales needed. That means instead of relying on every meeting to lead to a close, have four times as many meetings. And to ensure you really hit your revenue target, aim for two proposals for every one you need closed.

NUMBER OF SALES NEEDED
NUMBER OF SALES YOU NEED TO CLOSE PER WEEK

NUMBER OF PROPOSALS
PROPOSALS = NEW SALES x2

NUMBER OF MEETINGS
4 MEETINGS UNTIL PROPOSAL

NUMBER OF PROSPECTS
PROSPECTS = 10X # OF SALES

Because revenue is a lagging indicator of the work done, the only thing we need to measure and have complete control over is how many people with whom we are connecting on a weekly basis.

By measuring our booked meetings, we will learn how effective we are in securing meetings with prospects. And measuring the number of proposals will show us how effective we are at having converting high-value conversations.

The revenue will come if we are doing everything else correctly. If we connect with the right number of people, get the right number of meetings, put out the right number of proposals, and we still aren't getting the revenue, that means we need to either increase our numbers (at the end of the day, sales is just a numbers game) or become more effective and powerful in our interactions with our prospects.

Fill out your sales funnel and send me an email. I want to hear from you. Are the number of meetings and prospects with whom you need to connect something you can do? What do you need to help you achieve your goals faster?

Garth and His Call Tenacity

When I worked for Xerox, one of the best salespeople was a man named Garth. Garth was a socially-awkward character. He had a hard time keeping a steady conversation. His brain was always four steps ahead of everyone else's. He would come into the office with a wrinkled shirt all the time. And when we would jokingly ask if he owned, or even knew how to use, an iron, he would reply that he didn't need to. He took his shirt into the bathroom with him when he showered, and the steam took out most of the wrinkles. I thought to myself that if his shirt had only the minor wrinkles I saw, what was the crumpled mess his shirt had started out like?

But despite Garth's lack of presentation and his lack of being able to contribute to a standard conversation, he was also one of the best reps Xerox had at the time.

Garth was a great listener. He would ask meaningful questions. And he would always do the work.

Garth was relentless when it came to booking meetings. When he would call someone to ask for a meeting and they would say *no*, he would checkmark his piece of paper in front of him. And if you were passing by, you would hear him enthusiastically say to himself, "Nine more to go," and then, "Eight more to go," and so on.

When I asked him why he was so excited when he was rejected, he told me none of these responses were rejections. They were all just people telling him, "Not right now," and he would never lose a beat.

In sales, we told each other for every person who answers *no,* they're actually saying, *not right now*. The timing isn't right. And timing is everything when it comes to sales. We depend on budgets, on approvals, on current projects to be completed, for resources to be available or for vacation time to start or end. There are hundreds of factors we may need in order to move or start a sales cycle. But those who understand the timing was off in the single moment you called that one time will continue to call and will always get the sale in the end.

But Garth would instead count down the number of calls he needed to make a meeting. Instead of counting the number of *no's* he was receiving, which could become deflating after a while, he counted down to the *yes*. Now, it's not a perfect science. You're not going to get through none *no's* and then magically the next one will be *yes*, but it does mean it may take you that long to get to *yes*, so hang in there.

I borrowed Garth's method of counting down to the *yes*, and I was surprised how much more upbeat I was after the sixth or seventh rejection. When I was counting the number of refusals for a meeting, I felt I was slowly chipping away. Little by little.

Changing the game in my head was empowering, because every now and then, I wouldn't have to wait until call number nine before the next one became an agreement to meet. Sometimes it would happen on call six or four! Then I would celebrate. Yes! I got to the goal without having to go the entire way. And then I would start all over again.

Focus On The Goal

At American Express, it became harder to book meetings. I was no longer selling $40,000 printers; I was now selling $40M payment solutions. I was asking people to change the way they were processing their payments, which was a lot harder to do.

The people I called on were the Chief Financial Officers (CFOs) for major international conglomerates, or if I couldn't get through to them, I called on their Vice President of Finance. Oftentimes, I'd have to call 10 people inside one company hoping to get the meeting. At times this required some fancy word play, because when I did get in touch with someone at one of these companies and they tried to refer me to someone else who'd already said no, I worked to convince them why they were still the person with whom I needed to meet. Why would I do that? Because if I met with just one person in the organization, I'd ask that person more questions about their company and get to know their processes, systems and the things they were striving for as an organization. None of this information could be found on a website. The more insight I had into the company, the more I could structure new conversations about how our service would impact their company on a larger, more positive level. But I needed to get the meeting first.

So, with the many times that I would call inside one company, it was common to go through many more calls which ended in, "Not right now, thanks." But I would persevere.

After a particularly bad month, I finally shook it all off. I said to myself: *You are going to keep calling people until you make your meeting targets.* It was a Friday afternoon. And with all the excuses salespeople and entrepreneurs tell ourselves, one of the most common ones is, "Don't call on a Friday. No one wants to receive a call to book a meeting." This one is complete garbage. One of my best days for making successful phone calls were Fridays before a long weekend. Most people had already left the office for the weekend, and the only person left, including to answer the phones, were the higher-ups, the decisionmakers.

So I called.

And I called more.

I was at my 15th rejection. And I kept telling myself to dig a bit deeper. Call another. The next one had to be *yes*.

Finally, after 16 calls, I connected with someone who said, "Sounds good. Looking forward to meeting."

I was elated! All that hard work had paid off.

But what did I do next?

I didn't stop. Because now I was on call 17. And if sales 101 is an accurate guideline, I would only have to make three more calls to get to my next *yes*.

I didn't have to make three more. The next person I called also said *yes*. I was now officially done for the day.

If you manage the tasks you need to do on a weekly basis—making phone calls, booking meetings and sending proposals, the revenue will always come.

Never take your foot off the prospecting accelerator. You may be having a couple of great months. The money is coming in consistently. Clients are finding you through amazing methods and so you start to slow down. Prospecting is a lot of work, and since the revenue is here, why spend all that energy prospecting more? Consistent prospecting will be something you notice the results of, maybe not right away, or even 60 days from today, but you will notice it. In 90 days, when there isn't any revenue coming through, it will be because of the lack of action three months ago, not because of what you're doing today.

As you grow your business and decide to hire new employees, this will also be something to watch for. Many people believe bringing on even slightly experienced salespeople is the answer to all their worries about revenue generation. But what are the metrics and the targets on which you will be measuring them? What if revenue isn't enough? They must also ensure they hit their targets for calls made and meetings booked.

And if you're reading this book, thinking you just want to know what to do and don't want to take action as a part of the revenue generation team? You're sadly missing the point.

I've met with plenty of entrepreneurs and business owners. They're wonderfully passionate people. They love their business and what they want to achieve, but for some reason there are some who don't want to be the leading salesperson in their company. "I'll hire someone else to do that."

Now I've been through my fair share of cyclical economies. I know that there are great times—bullish markets and spending is happening freely. There are also down times—the bearish market, recessions and depressions. I have seen companies grow from one to 10, 15, and 100 people in short periods of time. I have also seen those same companies lose half their staff because of the loss of revenue.

You may be fortunate to have hired others to help you become responsible for revenue generation, but the only one who's accountable for the revenue coming in is you, the business owner.

Set a good example. Tell your team what you expect of them. Help them develop great habits, because it's worked for you.

And even when your team becomes so large that you are doing less of the revenue generation, it doesn't mean you should do none. When I worked for companies such as Xerox and American Express, even the President and Vice Presidents of those organizations had their own sales targets to achieve and clients to manage. Revenue generation should be everyone's responsibility.

Now we're starting to see that shift to more companies becoming first and foremost sales companies. Companies are empowering their staff to have more client relationships. I've seen manufacturers train their delivery personnel to know how to question their clients more effectively. Delivery people are seen as reliable and the people to whom they deliver have great relationships with them. When a delivery person asks a question, you're almost always receiving honest answers. Imagine how powerful it would be if a delivery person was asking the right questions and relayed back to you or your sales team if there was a new opportunity to sell one of your new products or services.

Xerox used to train their service technicians in the same way, and as a sales rep for the company, some of the biggest leads I received were from the people who were directly working with the client in different ways.

When I spoke to the founders of Barefoot Wineries, they said they trained the receptionist through the warehouse people and were amazed with some of the revenue-generating suggestions that came from these empowered employees.

Sales skills and helping to generate leads should be the responsibility of every person who has an interaction with the client, not just the salesperson.

Money is a Flow-Through

I work with a lot of entrepreneurs and solopreneurs (those entrepreneurs who prefer to keep their ventures as a single-person operation). In the first conversation I ask the person, "What is your goal for the end of the year?" They will usually start out with something vague, such as "I want more customers," or, "I want to feel like my company is a success." The struggle with these vague goals is how do you measure them and how do you know when you've achieved them?

One time I had someone tell me they only wanted to "make more money." I went into my purse and pulled out a

$20 bill. I put in on the table and told them I was happy to provide, and that would be my normal coaching rate of thousands of dollars. The person choked. I had a good laugh. The point had been made. I helped them make more money. But without clarification and quantification on what that actually means, how do you know when you've achieved your goal?

You can have many specific goals, but please ensure you also have a well-defined a financial goal.

It doesn't matter if you are a business owner or a salesperson working for a company. You need to define your financial goal, because this is one of the areas which measures both the success and the tasks that need to be done in order to achieve the goal. Revenue gives us the ability to reverse-engineer the goal to determine how we are going to get there.

For instance, saying you *want more customers* as your goal:
How many customers do you want?
How much do you want each customer to spend?
How will you ensure your current customers aren't reducing their spend while bringing on new ones?
And the questions go on.

When we choose revenue to be our target, we use our average value of each customer and we determine how many customers in total with whom we need to be working. From there, we can use Sales 101 standard metrics of 10 prospects per customer to determine the number of prospects with whom we need to be engaging on a monthly or weekly basis.

Usually at this point, someone will tell me they aren't motivated by money.

And I get it. If you currently have a bad relationship with money, with limiting beliefs and self-talk such as, *money is the root of all evil*, or you had a parent who was always chasing the dollar and didn't appreciate the people around them, this could be a hard thing to set your target on.

But you're right. It's not about the money. It's about what the money can do for you.

Money is a flow-through to greater opportunities in your life.

With money, we can tell the marketplace how to value us (unfortunate but true). People don't value the things they get for free, but they do value the things (and experiences) for which they have to pay.

The other reality is money makes the world go around. So, when we determine our full worth, people understand it and are willing to invest in it, and we have the means to help even more people.

It takes money to bring on a marketing campaign that allows more people to understand our message and impact. It takes money to hire more people so we can impact a larger chunk of the industry or the world. It takes money to publish books, travel to new geographies and do the things that many industry leaders are doing.

If we're not motivated by money, then it's time to become motivated.

Because when money is coming in, we get to help more people. We get to impact a larger part of the world.

I know when my company is successful. I have more students enrolling in our program. We have more attendees at our networking events. I get to hire more staff and provide them with a life, a career and a way to positively affect more business owners. We have the opportunity to invest in better events and share our message with even more people who are looking for a better way to connect with their customers.

The students who do invest with us learn the processes and strategies to navigate a high-value sale. This allows them to receive more revenue, hire people, invest more in their product or service and help more of their customers do amazing work better.

The single dollar that comes into our organization is not just the one-dollar bill. It has the ability to multiple. And as it flows through us, its impact on everyone who it affects provides its true impact on the world.

Yes, money may not be the goal, but it is something we can measure.

It's not about making the money. It's about how it flows through you to help others.

How does the money a client invests in you, your company and your service flow through you? Do you hire a marketing company? Ultimately help the owner of that company live a better life for their family? Do you hire employees who now have a career they love and a financial wellbeing they can provide for their family? Or perhaps the profits or commission you make from the sale ultimately allow you to take your family on the vacation of your dreams?

Chapter Five

The Evolving Sales Cycle

Many people have a negative impression of what sales is because they're still caught up in the idea that sales is a greasy, pushy ploy to get someone to buy what they have. As if sales is about manipulation and coercion to force someone to buy something that doesn't work and yet promises to be everything. This is the *snake-oil* sales process—selling a product that no one wanted or needed, and yet somehow people bought because of all the false promises it made. A man stood on a wooden soap box at the fair plugging his cure-all potion. This played out later with the impression we have of the discount used-car salesperson who says whatever he has to in order to get you to buy that lemon. It was the "I have it," and, "You need it," and the person could inflate the price to whatever the market would bear.

There is little to this type of sale.

The prospect knows they have a problem, and before the days of Internet and easily-accessible research, there was little the prospect could do to find the solution to their problem on their own. They could go to the library and read up on any topic they desired, but many chose to skip that step and go directly to the seller, trusting that person to be honest. They'd hear what they needed to firsthand, and then make a decision from there, oftentimes making their decision quicker than they felt comfortable with because the salesperson used a pressure technique such as, "This is our last one," or, "There is another buyer coming in within an hour."

This type of sales process still does exist, but those who use it will not be in business for very long because with the power of social media and online reviews, people will not stand for it. We are protective of others and want to ensure any person in which we are doing business is ethical and reputable in their delivery of their promises.

The Challenger Model

As technology took over and Internet forums became available, buyers met in online communities to read the experiences of others. It was not enough for the salesperson just to push their product to the buyer. The buyer needed to be convinced *before* connecting with the seller that they were interested in potentially purchasing.

Oftentimes, unless the client *knew* they had a problem, there was nothing for which to search. The Challenger model fixed this by focusing on the problem the client might potentially be facing. In simplistic terms, the salesperson approached the client and started the conversation with, "Do you suffer from this...?" The client, now in agreement, became more receptive to hear what the salesperson wanted to offer as a solution to a problem they'd only recently discovered was a problem.

The Challenger Model focused on the problems the client had. It focused on the consequences of these problems, and in a way became the new method for salespeople who wanted to set themselves apart as the new trusted advisor. Gain trust first in the pain and then provide a solution to that problem.

The salesperson became well versed in asking:
Do you suffer...?
What is your challenge?
What pain keeps you up at night?
And so on. The intention being that as long as the salesperson focused on the pain and suffering of the client, there was always something to fix. That pain was conveniently fixed by purchasing the seller's product or service.

Unfortunately, as information became more prevalent, the Challenger model did not age well. Buyers no longer needed their salespeople to inform them of their problems. They had the Internet. If they had a problem, they could source the solution online.

WebMD became the most recognizable solution provider in this space, and in effect, most websites mimicked that level of information. The Internet became a jungle of symptoms and diagnoses. When a patient went to the WebMD site, they filled out their symptoms, checking boxes and reading the little info popups. Whether they were suffering from a certain symptom or not, occasionally hypochondria set in and boxes were selected *just to be safe.*

After seven minutes filling out an online survey the patient, got a printout of all the possible issues from which they could be suffering, the most serious at the very top. Then the patient went to their doctor's office with a 15-page printed document and told the doctor they already knew what they needed and to prescribe them the specific pharmaceutical listed in the report.

Today, our clients are no different. Unless we are approaching them for the first time and they have no idea they have a specific problem, they have already self-diagnosed themselves with the source of their challenges and have searched out, or sourced WikiHow, to find the most appropriate Band-Aid fix.

When we approach our clients for the first time with the problem-centric model, the answer we most typically get is that "there is no problem." Because there really isn't. *If it ain't broke, don't fix it.* If it was a real problem, they would already have done something about it. The problem they are facing may be big, but the solution they were able to source took too much time, cost too much money or became more involved than it was worth. The client likely decided the problem wasn't big enough to have solved.

How do you help someone who doesn't have a problem? You can't. You can spend energy trying to convince someone of a problem they really don't believe they have or you can completely change the conversation.

Goal-Based Selling

In the new sales conversation, we move away from the client's problems and focus on their goals and aspirations.

A conversation based around the client's goals and aspirations becomes product-and-service independent. We question the client about where they want to be in the future. And although we may talk about five or 10 years in the future, many clients use those goals as a guideline as opposed to a specific plan. We are most interested in the short-term goals: six months to a maximum of two years. Short-term goals are tangible. We can help someone get there easily. We provide feedback and advice and help direct a plan to get the client to their goals faster.

Goal-Based Selling is the epitome of working with someone on creating a relationship. Buyer and seller relationship aside, when we connect with someone in our lives, in our own personal relationships, the reason we choose to date and eventually marry one person over another is because they best align with our goals. Our dreams and ambitions match with what the other person desires and we believe by working together with that person we will get there faster.

When we start our sales conversation, we will surround our questions around the topic of, "Where do you want to be in six months?" and, "What would this look like for you?"

Every client should have some goals for themselves or their business. If they don't, why are they here?

As the client tells us their goals, our job is not to jump right away into how we can help them, but rather understand the impact of not getting there, what that would mean for their business and why *now* achieving their goal is important to them. We cannot help anyone until they are motivated to act.

Only after we understand the ramifications of someone not achieving their goal can we then move to how our product or service will help them to get there faster.

Example of Goal-Based Selling

I provide my calendar booking link in almost every email I send. I encourage anyone to book me and I am happy to provide phone call support in whatever the person is struggling with in getting more sales and ultimately achieving their goals.

My next meeting is with a woman named Ashley.

Ashley tells me how she is currently working as a day-home operator but no longer wants to do that. What she dreams about is starting another business—one where she is doing professional photography for businesses. She dreams of going into an office and taking corporate headshots and office environment shots which will be used for websites and promotional materials.

"How soon do you want that to become a reality?" I ask her.

"As soon as possible," she replies.

"What would you like your business to be producing in six months? Dollars? Clients? Types of work?" I dig further.

"I would love to be making my day-home income in six months. Right now, I'm bringing in $3600 a month. I don't know how many clients that would be, but if I was charging $600 per client, I would need six per month," she replies.

Her response is not uncommon for when I am helping people uncover their dreams and turning it into an action plan the first time. Ashley is dreaming, but she's dreaming too small. She could easily charge more than $600 per client, especially if she's doing an entire company's headshots and other photography for promotional materials. But I don't jump into that topic just yet. Goal-based selling starts off entirely about the client and how they picture their dreams evolving. Ashley has spent some time thinking about her reality. I don't want to provide her with too many new ideas until I fully understand the dream she's created.

"And what would being able to do only photography do for you and your family?" I question.

People dream of a better life, not just for themselves, but because of the impact it will have on others. Many of us dream about the impact on our families, whether that is to provide them better lives, be home more or give them experiences such as traveling that we've wanted for ourselves, and by default for our loved ones. Other people dream of the impact they will be providing to the world. The legacy they would like to leave for others. I want to know how many more people their dreams touch. What would it mean to affect that many people in the ways one can imagine?

It's easy to give up on a dream when the only person we may potentially disappoint is ourselves. If we try and fail, it's okay, no one needs to know. If we've committed to others and try, failure becomes less of an option and also harder to admit.

"I would be able to attend my children's field trips if I wasn't running the day-home," she says. "And I would be a happier mother to my children."

Now we're getting somewhere.

"And how would that make you feel?" I ask.

I hear the sound of her deep breath. "Then life would be… *perfect…*" she slowly lets out.

I am satisfied with that answer.

No longer am I trying to help her move her income from full-time day-home operator to full-time corporate photographer. I will actually impact her life in a bigger way. I am helping her be there more for her children. I am helping her create a perfect life in her head. That's much more valuable than just replacing income from one source to another.

Goal-based selling drives to the deepest levels of why we are helping the person. What does it ultimately mean to the other person when this is accomplished?

Ask more questions during the goal-discovery portion of the meeting. They will always be your guiding light. When the client becomes confused on eventually taking action to move forward in a deal, remind them not just of their goals, but the reasons and the impact those goals will have on their lives.

The KO Advantage Sales Cycle

The sales cycle we've created and promote with our students is broken down into six simple steps.

The first five steps cover the sales cycle to get the first deal, with the sixth step covering what to do after the sale is made. After all, the best champions of your business are current and previous clients who are standing on the mountaintop singing your praises.

Although the title of each stage of the sales cycle is based on what you need to focus on as the seller, below the title is the summary of where the buyer is on their own journey. Finally, there are a few tips on what, as the seller, you need to be clear before moving the sale into the next stage of the cycle.

The seller and buyer relationship is no different than any other relationship you may be in. You may try to push your own agenda, but it won't matter. If the person feels they are being pushed into something they aren't ready for, they will leave. We will know where we are based on where the buyer is in their own decision-making process.

Every relationship involves two parts. We cannot move forward until we are in agreement on where we are together and we're on the same page to achieve our goals faster.

But before we cover each of the stages on what to do as the seller in the relationship, let's recognize how our sales cycle will align with the buyer's journey. We will use the buyer as a reference point to navigate us to ask the right questions in order to move us along the path together.

The Sales Cycle & The Buyer's Journey

Follow-up & Referral
Experiencing the product.
Singing praises.
Ask for testimonials and referrals.
Build your tribe.

Closing the Sale
Negotiate and purchase
"Are you ready TODAY?"
Give and Take negotiations

Proposal
Intent to buy. Know their needs will

Suspec
Buyer (not) a
What is the l
interaction?

Lead Qu
Engagement
BANT: Budge
Timeline
What is the c

Value C
Interest and c

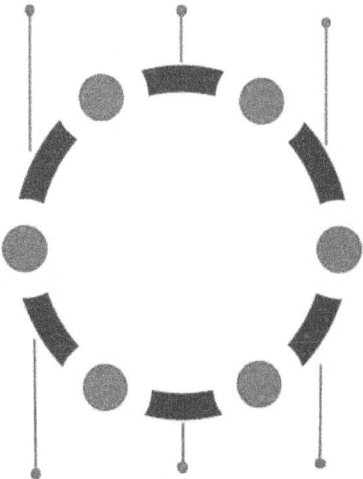

Chapter Six

The Buyer's Journey

Like all relationships, the buyer and seller have a two-part relationship.

Far too many sales books and trainings focus on just one part of that two-part relationship: the seller. But a relationship book would never focus only on one person in the relationship. It takes two. Only by knowing where the buyer is in their own journey can we as sellers have a better idea of where we are.

There will be times when we need to push the conversation along. There are plenty more times when we need to hold ourselves back and truly listen to the other party. What are they concerned about? What are they saying between the lines?

The sales cycle and process must include both the seller and the buyer to know where anyone is within this relationship. If we only wanted to focus on what the seller does, how you act and how to make the other person take action, then you're referring to manipulation or coercion. That is not sales. Sales serves the other person. It does not force.

Leading a sales cycle is taking the lead within a conversation. We become less like someone trying to pull a cat on a leash and more like a tour guide. If you've ever seen a cat being pulled on a leash, they often just lay down and become dead weight. If their owner thinks they're dead, maybe the leash will be taken off. On the other hand, a tour guide is much more inclusive in the conversation.

If you ever hire a tour guide for a museum tour, they typically do a great job of touching on the key points and helping you to move forward. They don't try to explain all the pieces in the museum or force you to get to the exit and gift shop the fastest. They walk you through each room, asking you to take special attention to a couple of select pieces. You are welcome to explore more yourself, knowing any questions can be taken back to the tour guide, who will do their best to answer them for you. Then, when you're ready, the tour guide will lead you to the next room in the museum.

It's not a rushed process. There is a timeline associated with it. Most museum tours won't go on endlessly. But there is direction. There is focus. And although, as the museum patron, you feel as if you are in charge of the speed and the direction, the museum tour guide knows they are in charge. They just allow you the space to feel as if you have the opportunity to explore on your own.

The buyer is on their own journey. Although we want them to feel as if they are in complete control, the moment they decide to engage you, it becomes the fine art between allowing them to explore on their own and leading them along. We need to respect the buyer while they are on their own journey.

The buyer will go through many phases throughout their journey. In the very beginning, if we are approaching them for the first time, they may become aware there is a better way of doing what they've been able to do. When the buyer reaches out to you as the vendor for the first time, they likely know they have a problem and there is a better way of doing things and are seeking a solution. Then they collaborate with others to see who (or what) can solve their problem the fastest, cheapest or easiest. Once they have determined a solution is out there, they will challenge the fit, purchase and then experience the product or service.

Review The Buyer's Journey

Aware — Seek — Collaborate — Challenge — Buy —

Aware of a Problem	Seek a Solution	Involve Others	Challenge of Fit	Purchase
Get them to agree they have a challenge, or that the challenge is within their future	Start the process of sourcing possible solutions that can be performed internally or externally	Begin the process of involving third parties into the discussion to find the best solution	Buyer looks internally if the solutions the third parties are presenting are as good as they claim	Buyer has made a decision based on the best fit for their organization. This is either choosing a solution internally or

Awareness

We all know about what we are knowledgeable, whether that is because we studied it in school, were taught it by our family, friends, or colleagues or we took time to learn it, such as and education or hobby.

Then there is a whole area of the things about which we know we don't know. For example, knowing another language exists but not knowing how to speak or read it, or knowing someone can study the discipline of aerodynamics and not know more than that when it comes to it.

Finally, there is what is called the unconscious unconsciousness. This is the area of knowledge about which we know nothing and don't know it exists. These are the things we learn for the very first time. This is the largest area of knowledge there is. There are far more things we don't know, and know nothing about, than what we do know.

Many of our prospects will fall into this area before we ever have our first conversation with them. They don't know there is a better way of doing business, not because they haven't found the answer, but because they are completely unaware that the way they are doing business is not the best way of doing it. They are unconsciously unconscious.

During our initial conversation with the client, we want to encourage creativity and start with where they are by asking, "How could you do this better?"

When we ask questions such as, "Do you know there is a better way?" the prospect may immediately become defensive. No one wants to be told they are not smart enough to know there is a better way. No one wants to be called ignorant in not knowing there was another possibility out there. Besides, if there was an easier way of doing what they are doing, they likely would have sourced it out and found it.

Awareness is where we initiate the conversation. This will be your initial phone calls and introductory emails. This could be some form of inbound marketing, but those conversations often take a longer time to evolve. In sales, we typically initiate the conversations with the companies with which we want to do business. This isn't to say that we choose not to do business with companies or individuals who reach out to us, but rather, when we start the conversation, we are more likely to educate the client first. We will provide them with the most accurate information, not information provided by inaccurate websites, or competitors who are more interested in the financial transaction than the long-term client relationship.

Seek a Solution

As we grow our business, release more content, update the website and move more into educating our consumers, we will begin to have more prospective clients reach out to us. This could be from web searches which land on your website and submit a request through the *contact us* form or it could be from referrals and word of mouth. But by the time the client reaches out to you for the first time, they have an awareness of what they need to grow their business and it could potentially be provided by you and your company.

This does not mean it is a done deal. Rather, this is just the beginning of the larger conversation. We must get to know from the prospect what they already know about us, the solution they believe we can provide and what the prospect believes will change in their lives/businesses when we are done doing business with each other.

But likely this consumer is seeking information from multiple vendors. Rarely does a prospect learn of the first company, even one with a glowing review, and not do more research on other vendors out there. They will begin to compare costs, time investments, comprehensiveness of solutions and reviews from others.

Know where you stand and where you compete and own that with pride. Don't automatically assume the client is looking for something else. Don't tell yourself the prospect is looking for the best price. That's almost never the case. Your strength is knowing at what you excel and charging the right price for it.

At KO Advantage Group we do a lot of public speaking. We are hosted at various events throughout North America and speak on how to create premium relationships with clients. We may adjust the particular area of focus within the sales cycle and conversation, but it will always cover how to create valuable relationships which lead to higher-paying clients and more personal attention.

Jacob attended one of my events. He had been spending the last few months learning more about marketing and how to create interest in his website, ads and other means of bringing new interest into his business. Then one of his friends mentioned to him that maybe what he really needs isn't more leads but a method of closing those conversations. Maybe he should look into sales skills.

Jacob was one of the first people to come up to me after my talk. He said he had started looking for sales strategies a week ago, and it felt like perfect timing when he saw my talk listed. I agreed to give him a call later that week and we could discuss more about what he was looking for.

We had a great call. We talked about his business. We spoke about his goals and how having a sales process and strategy would help him get there faster. Then I asked him the question to test where he is in his decision-making process on the right sales education for him. "What do you need to make your decision?"

He responded that since he was just in the beginning stages he wanted to look more at my program and one other. I asked him what other program that might be. He provided me the name of the other company. I knew of them. They offered a product a third of the price of ours. They used a completely different business model. Instead of having small classes meet in an online video chat with their instructor as we do, the other company required people to attend four-hour sessions in person once a week. For me, this made no sense. If the person was having to give up a majority of their day to learn to sell, when would they actually take the time to do the selling? And most importantly, we were willing to back up our claims. We provided a *Results Guaranteed* clause in the contract. And as far as I knew, no one else in this space had a guarantee as in-depth as ours.

We chatted about each one of these differences and why it was important as a business owner to choose the best solution for his company—not the cheapest or the fastest, but rather the one that was going to support his sales strategy and growth as he built.

Jacob wasn't anywhere close to making a decision. And if I was to push him to decide today, I would likely lose him as a client forever. He was trying to determine what would be best for his business knowing he needs a solution today. Could he get by with cheap and fast training which he knows isn't perfect but may be "just enough" to get him to the next phase? Or should he decide to go for the larger investment— financially and time wise, and *know* he is getting the right solution?

What I did was continue to talk to Jacob. We agreed I would call him in a couple of weeks and continue our conversation. The best I could hope for with Jacob would be to move him to a collaboration phase. I continued to talk to him about his business and goals, product and service aside, and became a trusted advisor in the process.

Collaborate

At the collaboration phase, the prospect starts to open up and become more honest (if honesty is one of their values) about what they are seeking and how they believe it will impact their business. If the prospect is not honest with you at this point in the conversation, it is up to you to decide whether you want to continue the conversation and feed their ego, or if you are more interested in helping those who better align with your own values.

In the collaboration phase, you should feel as if the client is opening up to you. The questions you ask are being received with open and transparent answers, no matter how difficult the answers are to hear. And this is where the magic starts to happen.

When we collaborate with the client, we are creating the best solution for that client *together*. We may already know what we're able and not able to do for them, but every client is unique and wants to feel their unique needs will still be addressed in the standard solution being created for them. If you are completely customizing the solution for your client, you will need to understand from their perspective what may go wrong, what they are most concerned about and how the solution they are ultimately seeking will help them achieve their goals faster.

The collaboration phase in the buyer's journey aligns with the value creation phase in the sales cycle. A majority of your sales cycle will be in this coinciding area.

Challenge

As the sales cycle moves forward and the prospect becomes closer to making a decision, new questions from the buyer will arise. This is where the prospect begins to challenge the fit. Objections may include:

How much will it cost?

Can you do it for cheaper?

How fast will it be completed?

What happens if it doesn't work?

What guarantees do you have in place?

Who else have you worked with?

And so on.

This is a good sign. It means you are closer to getting the deal. But it's not done yet.

This is an important process for the buyer. They are on the fence. They are close to deciding and want full confirmation that this is the right decision for them. Some people will need more assurance than others, but what they are ultimately asking is *will you be there for me when I need you?*

Objections are best answered with additional questions and understanding from where the concern from the client is stemming. I have seen deals lost because for every objection, the salesperson or business owner had a perfectly-scripted response.

With this type of response, you may end up moving the prospect from feeling you understand their unique needs to, "I have an answer for everything." Scripted responses make your client feel as if you receive these objections all the time. They feel as if, "I'm not the only one who is concerned about this," which may play in your favor or against it.

When the prospect begins to challenge the fit, the best place to go is back to questions. What will make them feel comfortable to move forward? Why is that a concern for them? Where is this concern stemming from?

Once you've addressed their concerns, move away from following the client's lead on where their comfort is, to now giving them a slight nudge. It's time to ask for the deal.

What will it take for you to say *yes* today?

Buy

The buying process for the client includes the proposal stage, the signing of the contract and the initial implementation.

The prospect may be in buying stage with more than one vendor. This is because they still haven't made their full decision yet and are hoping for some golden moment in one of the proposals where the best answer will be provided.

If you are up against multiple vendors, or even just one other party, understand how the buyer will be making their decision. Ask them:

How will they know they made the right decision?

By what will they be judging the different solutions? How will they know the solution they picked worked? And how will they be measuring those results? Price aside, what else is important in making this decision? How will those factors be ranked in importance?

If a client answers me that they are most concerned about price and then other factors after that, I will try my best to push them back to the collaboration phase. I know I am not the cheapest solution, and chances are you chose to read this book because you aren't either. Solution providers like us don't compete on price. We will always lose. And I'm okay with losing that battle.

I will ask the client, "Why did you choose the vendors you did to compare against?" And if that doesn't get them to start changing their mind, I will press on, "What's more important? The cheapest price up front or maximizing the return on your investment?" And the *return on investment* should be clarified before this point in time. This will be covered further in the chapter Determining Return on Investment.

When you are at the proposal stage, the proposal is as much a part of the buying process as the contract signing. This is your client's first opportunity to see and feel what it will be like to have you as a partner as they continue to grow their business.

Once the client makes the decision to go with you, it becomes about stepping up and showing them the absolute best experience their money could buy.

Be there early, quickly and often with the answers they seek. Do your best to step above and beyond, because referrals don't typically come immediately after the client has bought, but rather after their experience of working with you and your product or service.

Experience

This is the moment where your client has been working with you, experiencing your product or service and is now ready to stand on the mountaintop and sing your praises.

The deal isn't done when the contract is signed. The deal is done after the service has been delivered and the client has agreed to provide you with a testimonial. That's the true reflection on whether you have done an exceptional job.

As you continue to grow your business, spend more time and energy asking yourself:

How can we create a better customer experience?

How do we make the onboarding easier?

How do we provide our clients with even more value for the price they are paying?

How do we make it easy to increase the number, quality or impact of the testimonials our clients are providing us?

When you make the experience seamless, future sales cycles, marketing initiatives and sourcing new clients, all of it, becomes easier.

And when you're ready to expand into new products or services, your current and former clients will be the first ones to whom you will be able to go. They will be the ones most likely to buy and the ones who will give their honest feedback on how you can make it even better.

Chapter Seven

There's no such Thing as a "Born Salesperson"

When I was pregnant, it was an exciting time. For the first couple months of pregnancy I was convinced my husband and I were going to have a baby girl. My whole family is women. I grew up with two sisters and four cousins (three of whom are women), two aunts, and multiple extended family—again, all women.

My husband, on the other hand, was the complete opposite, with more males on his side of the family, and he was convinced having anything besides a boy was not even a possibility.

So, for weeks I read online all the old wives' tales—what cravings I was having, whether my skin was looking better or worse since becoming pregnant and where the moon had been positioned at our time of conception. All of this was to try to prove to my husband that we were, in fact, having a girl and not a boy.

The 20th week of pregnancy is the anatomy scan by the ultrasound technician. Besides checking for healthy limbs and cranial growth, they can also tell you the sex of the baby. Finally, one of us would be right in our *knowing* of what our little baby would be.

As the ultrasound technician smoothed the gel over my belly and scanned along, my husband and I held hands. Would she tell us we're having a little baby boy or a little baby girl? Will it be a little baby Kim wearing cute pink dresses, or a baby Shawn wearing chic vests and bowtie combos?

As the ultrasound technician scanned my belly, at no time did we expect her to pause, take a deep breath and say, "Kim, Shawn, you're not having a little baby boy or a little baby girl…you're going to have a salesperson!"

Being a salesperson is not something into which you're born. It's not something you either possess or don't have. It's a skill. It's like learning to read, ride a bike or learning to cook. It's a series of steps. A process you follow. And like any skill, it can be really hard and difficult at the beginning, and as you continue to practice it and get better at it, you can start to do it naturally.

Although my husband and I both had successful sales careers and now own our own businesses, our boy Marcus may end up being a better negotiator when it comes to his grades with his teachers. But that is because he learned and practiced that skill.

Sales Skills take Time

When I cooked my first turkey for Christmas dinner, I went online and found a recipe. I bought all the ingredients, and on Christmas Day, I finally read the recipe.

Step 1: To create the brine, combine the aromatic herbs, citrus and stock in a pot.

Yes, I can do this.

Step 2: Bring to a boil.

So far so good.

Step 3: Allow to brine to cool then cover turkey with brine and refrigerate for 24-48 hours.

Oh, crap.

I hadn't read the recipe the first time. But I did what I could do. I stuffed the turkey and used the brine as the base as it roasted. I underestimated how long it would take for the turkey to cook, and the turkey was done two hours after the rest of the meal was prepared.

Was it the best turkey? Probably not. My family was likely too generous with the compliments. But the following year I was better prepared. I made the brine a couple of days ahead and marinated the turkey for the recommended time.

The third year, the turkey was finished roasting 30 minutes before the rest of the meal.

The fourth year, I adjusted the recipe slightly to better match my taste preferences.

Each time I followed the recipe, I got a little bit better. The end result continuously became better. And my skills in cooking a turkey improved year after year.

What would have happened in that first year if I'd decided to quit the moment realized I didn't marinate the turkey for the 24 hours the recipe asked for? Should I have thrown my hands up in the air? I could have gone to my husband and said, "I tried to cook a turkey, and it didn't work. I give up!" Of course not. That would be a waste of a turkey. It would have been a disappointment to my family and friends who were counting on me. They were still impressed that I tried, even if it wasn't perfect.

But people do this when they are trying to make a sale.

They will freeze in the first step of sales process. That could be the initial call for a meeting, a LinkedIn request or sending an email to connect.

They send one and never get the result they are after, so they decide to completely give up. "This process doesn't work, Kim."

Or worse, they never make that first phone call because they are so concerned about trying to say the perfect first thing over the phone that they never attempt the call.

I knew a woman who would agonize about making the phone call.

She was in **KO Sales U** and after we taught her the lesson on making phone calls, she froze. We show the students the formula for creating a great phone call. We do not provide a call script. Instead, we give the outline of a call and ask for the student to add their own message and authenticity into the mold. We require students to practice their phone call conversation with their fellow students. One of the requirements to passing the program is completing a certain number of role plays with their classmates. This woman refused to do it.

When I asked her where she was in drafting her first phone call conversation and how soon she would be ready to practice, she always needed more time.

But after a month, she still hadn't started.

When I followed up with her again she said she was still trying to figure out the perfect thing to say.

I knew if she wasn't forced to do this it would never happen, so I told her to stop thinking about the perfect thing to say and just start talking.

Then I made her pretend to call me.

Despite us having a 10-minute conversation up until this point, the moment I asked her to pretend to call me, her anxiety spiked. What was once an articulate woman became a blubbering mess. She stuttered over her words. She would say one thing and then stop herself and ask for a second to rephrase it. She sounded as if she was close to crying on the phone.

But she got through the fake phone call.

It was far from good. But she'd made her first attempt.

Then I told her to do it again.

The second time she was better. There was far less stuttering, and she didn't sound as if she was going to cry.

I made her do it a third, a fourth and a fifth time.

By the last time she practiced it, it was a night-and-day improvement. She didn't stop herself once. She went with the flow. She was even able to move through the objection of "send me some information."

Each time she practiced, she became better and better.

Because she was expecting to make the most perfect phone the very first time, she was setting her expectations up for failure. I have never met a single person who was able to try something for the first time and complete it to perfection.

Performance athletes have fallen, gotten hurt and bled before they ever became good enough to compete. Concert pianists likely started by jamming their fingers on a keyboard and eventually learning how to play Chopsticks. Even the best chefs in the world burnt their food when they were first learning.

Everyone started somewhere.

So have fun with it.

You will fail.

You will never complete the first time (or the second, or third…) the way you think it should be done in your head.

But you will get through it.

You will survive.

And you will learn from each experience and be able to do it a little bit better. Every. Single. Time.

Chapter Eight

Connecting with Your Prospects

It's always best to be the first one to start a conversation with new prospects, whether they are ready to buy right away or not. You become the educator on the topic. You often get to set the pace of the conversation. You are known as the person who brought awareness to a problem which had not been recognized before. And you help determine the best possible solution.

When clients come to you first, you don't know what information they've already received and from where they received it. You may have to battle preconceived notions about what your product or service offering actually is. You have to reset the conversation to focus on the impact of what the solution will provide and finally, what the reasonable expectations of final result are, whether they choose us or someone else.

One of our students in **KO Sales U** was a master at marketing and generating inbound leads. However, before he took **KO Sales U**, he was terrible at the sales conversation.

Prospects would contact James with questions about marketing services and online ad spend. The unfortunate reality was many of these prospects automatically believed spending money on Facebook ads and search engine optimization (SEO) generated guaranteed results. He would struggle to explain to his prospects that they may spend hundreds or thousands of dollars without generating a single client. Some understood. Many more believed what they saw online from people posting statuses in their network and thought James wasn't good enough. James's first objection he had to overcome in his sales cycle was getting prospects not to believe all the Facebook status hype that every dollar spent would automatically generate four in return. James would often lose the deal before ever getting an actual meeting.

You may have to spend one, two or even more meetings navigating the client toward what are real expectations versus any promises made from other unrealistic sources.

When I worked for American Express, we dealt with a wide variety of clients, the most common being government agencies and international conglomerations. Because of the size of our transactions, we often had to compete in a Request for Proposal (RFP) process.

When an RFP came out it, was a multi-page document which asked a series of questions about our products and services, checkboxes whether we did certain things or not and then finally the price.

When we met with a client before the RFP was released, we would have several conversations about what made us different and why those features were important to that particular client.

When the RFP was then released, we could easily see the impact of these conversations as certain questions were written in specifically for us to answer positively. Our initial conversations had impact.

If we weren't involved with the client before the RFP was released, we could oftentimes tell which vendor was helping to craft this conversation. There were certain questions which felt directed specifically for them.

We made a conscious decision as a team to no longer respond to RFPs if we were not involved in the conversations before the RFP was released. It was a difficult decision. After all, as Wayne Gretzky said, "You miss 100% of the shots you don't take."

RFPs would take a minimum of a full work week to put together. That was time well-spent if we had a great chance of winning, but it was a massive risk if we didn't. In that same week we could move other deals forward and connect with new prospects. We also knew most companies required a minimum number of responses before they were allowed to reward a contract, and by responding to a riskier RFP we were helping the issuing company make a faster and easy decision to not choose us. By not responding, we might have a chance to connect with the company after their process failed and have conversations to see where we stood.

I'm not saying don't respond to *any* RFP if that is part of your business process. Oftentimes junior companies will respond to every RFP they can as an awareness tactic. The more they get their name out there, whether they win or not, is valuable time spent for them. But do become strategic with initial client engagement. If the first time an RFP issuing company hears of your company is through a cattle-call process, call it what it is. It's a method to get in touch with a prospect for the first time, and spend your time accordingly.

However, your company may be better suited spending that same amount of time connecting fresh with new prospects and carving your own conversations instead of fitting into theirs.

Calling, emailing and connecting on social media are great ways to make that connection. Just know what your chances are of getting the meeting with each method and spend your time strategically on the right ones at the right time.

To Call or Email?

When we cover calling for meetings in the **KO Sales U** program, people will often ask me if it's okay if they do the same thing with email.

Calling a person and trying to get them live is not the same as sending an electronic mail, hoping the three paragraphs of content is enough for the recipient to take the same high-level action.

Email, unlike connecting with someone on the phone, is considered a low-value touchpoint.

Think of what you do when you receive an email from a name you don't recognize. Chances are you will look at the name and the subject line, and unless something jumps out at you, you will likely immediately delete it. If you do open it and it doesn't look like something you recognize, you may also unsubscribe yourself from the email list and then never be contacted by that person or company again.

Our clients are no different.

Salespeople and business owners typically prefer to email because it seems "less invasive." Email feels like it will be "easier." But anything that may be easy also produces less results.

As an entrepreneur, a business owner and sales professional, you can choose the easy route or the one which will produce the biggest impact.

Email is a low-impact touchpoint for a client. It is far too easy to delete an email in an inbox. It is too easy to ignore it and never respond. Email should never be the number one method of communication with any prospect. It leaves too much out of the conversation.

For me, I would much rather push myself out of my comfort zone and get better results than to spend my time working on something which is going to take longer to get to the final goal.

However, don't think you shouldn't email at all when working to get connected with a prospect for the first time. Instead, email should be used strategically. It should be part of the one, two (and three) punch. Email should either be used to connect with someone first to let them know you will be calling them at a specific time or to connect with someone outside of respectable business hours.

If you do choose to send email, spend more time on the subject line than the body of the email.

Similar to the old philosophical question, if a tree falls in the woods and there is no one to hear it, does it make a sound? The same thought applies to email. If you write the perfect email with the best call-to-action, and no one opens it, does it really matter?

The email body should be sharp, direct and to the point. It should mimic the conversation you would have with the prospect over the phone.

Tell the prospect specifically why you reached out to them.

How will engaging with you impact the prospect's life?

What is the *specific* action you would like the person to take?

Specific action includes asking for a specific date and time you would like to meet. If your call to action isn't specific enough, you may risk getting caught up in an email abyss.

If the prospect opens your email, likes what you have to say and is willing to sit down for the conversation, they will respond to your generic question, "Are you available to meet sometime next week?" What your generic ask is actually doing is asking the prospect to please take some time to review your calendar and choose one of the various open time slots and choose the one that works best for them. This is a lot harder than it sounds, especially for people who have others manage their calendar. Or if the person is hoping you will come back with something more, they may simply respond, "Yes, I'm available."

What's the next move you make? Another email with a couple choices of dates? What if it takes you too long to respond back to their email and then they become busy and forget to respond back to you?

There are too many uncertainties that could stand in your way and break the momentum you've created with your prospect. And you haven't even had the opportunity to meet for the first time!

Emails, like calls, should not be overly-complicated. Keep them simple. Write one solid email and then copy and paste it over and over again. Change any specific pieces, such as why you directed the email to that person, but the rest of it (including the ask for a meeting date and time) can be the same, especially if you are sending out dozens of emails. You're going to have a lot more non-responses than people saying *yes*, so don't worry about becoming double-booked. It will rarely happen, and if it does, let the person know the time they selected time was just taken and ask for a phone number to choose the next best time. Remember, you are in control of this process.

You are going to send a lot more emails than you would phone calls before you get an initial response. Even with the very best, the average email open rate will be less than 40% (there are some specific email marketers who do claim amazing open rates of closer to 70%!). But it's not just about getting the email opened, it's about taking the next step and getting the person to commit to taking action. And that's where the percentages will drop, because as much as a third, and more likely closer to only 10% of the people who *do* open the email will jump at your offering to meet.

This is why many businesses push to grow email lists. It all comes down to a numbers game.

My email marketing campaigns average a 40% open rate, and those are people who have heard of me and have already said *yes*, we want to continue to hear from you. My cold emails, where I am sending to someone who has never heard of me before and I am making a request to meet, has a call-to-action response of closer to 10%. And that's coming from the expert in this space. My pure introduction phone call to response rate is closer to 40%, meaning out of every 10 calls to people who have never heard of me before, four of the calls will lead to someone saying "Yes, I would love to meet with you." With the same number of people I contact via phone versus email, I receive three more people agreeing to meet when I place the request over the phone. That's a much better return on investment for my time, and it will be for yours, too!

Using LinkedIn and other Social Media

LinkedIn has taken off significantly over the last couple of years as *the* tool to connect with more people, especially those who are in the business-to-business space. LinkedIn has made it easy to learn all about someone's work history and education and find all their contact details.

And yes, LinkedIn is a great way to connect with people you haven't met and with whom you would like to start a business relationship.

With any easier form of connection also comes an easier way of ignoring or not responding to requests. The same way emails are naturally ignored (and deleted), the same goes for LinkedIn requests.

I have seen a lot of information out there that recommends always submitting a personalized request when requesting to connect with someone on LinkedIn. And I would agree with that for the people you purposefully want to connect with— those individuals you plan on calling or emailing in the future or have called in the recent past. But go in not expecting a response.

LinkedIn makes it too easy to accept (or decline) a request. And if you do choose to put in a personalized message when sending a request, that message now moves into the recipient's message folder so the recipient may follow up immediately after accepting your request. But changes are constantly happening. And what may work today may not work tomorrow.

Oftentimes, though, people are accepting LinkedIn requests during a busy time in their day and completely forget to respond.

Therefore, LinkedIn should be used with the intention that you want people to start recognizing you. They see your name and aren't entirely sure where they saw it, and then when you do call they are more likely to accept it because your name is now familiar.

When I place a LinkedIn request, with the limit to the customized request note field, I get right to business.

Tell the person the reason you want to connect with them. This is typically your elevator pitch question. And then close it with a call-to-action. Is it a meeting you want? Is it a call? Let the person know what you want them to do. Then leave all your expectations at the door.

LinkedIn and all other social media is a pure numbers game. You have to do a lot of it to get the responses you are asking for. When someone *does* respond to you, remember there is a person on the other end. Get to know them, and connect with them through a phone call, Skype or in-person meeting as quickly as possible.

Use social media as an extra tool in your tool kit, not as the *only* tool in your tool kit. You will never be able to build your business as fast as you like if you're not willing to step outside your comfort zone and make the phone calls, reach out to more people and let them know why working with you will change their world.

What is Your Intention?

Whatever method you use to reach out to a prospect the very first time, ask yourself—what is your intention in reaching out to them? What do you hope to get? How will you know it was successful?

Before reaching out to any prospect, and even throughout later meetings, always ask yourself, "What is my intention?"

When I am speaking on stage, I love asking the audience, "What's the intention of a cold call?"

Usually I get responses such as, "To get to know more about the other business and then to get the other business interested in you," or "To sell your product or service," or "To learn more information," and so on. Occasionally, will I have one person in the audience who actually knows—to get the meeting.

That's it.

The intention of the initial call is nothing more than to get the meeting.

Unless you are a pure phone salesperson, then your goal may be to make the sale, but I doubt you will do that with an initial outreach to someone who wasn't expecting your call.

Almost all companies have websites, and if some information is lacking from their website, you can check out what is on their social media accounts. If the company is small or privately held, there may not be nearly as much information available as their larger, publicly-traded counterparts, in which case, you can use competitive information to get an understanding about the industry landscape and of what the smaller company may need to be aware.

But all of that aside, there is only a single goal with the call (or email or social media reach out), and that is to book a meeting.

You cannot create high-impact relationships, and ultimately a high-impact sale, if you're not moving to high-impact connections, such as face-to-face meetings.

Later on, as we go through the rest of the sales cycle, the intention will be to understand if the prospect is qualified, or to determine how they will calculate their return on investment (ROI), or to clarify you have everything you need for the proposal and then ultimately close the deal.

Know what your intention is for every client interaction and then ask for it.

You're more likely to get what you want when you know what you want to get.

Chapter Nine

Calling for Meetings

I was working with a client to create a strategy to get more conversations with the people with whom she wanted to connect.

As we discussed calling new people, she told me she absolutely hated the idea of cold calling, and for her it wasn't about making cold calls. She was actually calling for meetings.

Cold Calling sounded so stark and there was so much fear associated with it. But in today's age, it's rare that we're doing *pure* cold calling anymore. We've done our research. We've reached out to more people via social media and other platforms. We have a better understanding about how we can help more individuals and businesses.

Calling for meetings was exactly what she was doing, which had less fear tied to it.

Going forward, find what works for you. Don't call the process something which incites fear or anxiety. Call it what you want. And call it something that makes sense. I've known people who will call it *the getting to know you call* or the *hi, I can help you with that* call.

Personally, I love naming it, "Calling for Meetings." It sets the intention of what you are wanting to achieve with the call. It focuses on the ideal outcome. And when things move in ways we aren't expecting, it brings us back to the ultimate goal—get the meeting.

You can't move any high-value conversation forward until you get an opportunity to meet with the client. You still need to understand their goals and aspirations and how they are building their business in order to achieve that quickly and efficiently. And you may not be able to do that in the initial phone call. However, calling for the meeting will likely lead to success. Whether that meeting is a booked in-person meeting, a video call or a booked phone call, once it's in both yours and the prospect's calendar, it exists and intention is set.

Why Do We Call?

Every relationship has to start somewhere.

As a sales professional, business owner or entrepreneur, that means we need to be making the first move. No one is going to know our product or service exists or that they even need us to help them out if we're not making those phone calls.

Too many people found comfort with email. It's easy. It feels non-invasive.

When we do cover emails, the goal is to craft a good email, change a line or two for each recipient, copy and paste and then blast off email after email.

There is definitely a time and place for emails, but if you are working to create a high-value conversation, then email is not it. Very few people who have ever read an email are responding and booking meeting times with you, unless your email is so compelling they are interested. Don't rely on email.

The phone call is a lost art. It's the connection we create with people. Only face-to-face is a better opportunity to understand someone completely, but the phone call is the next best thing. Why do you think most people send an email asking for the phone meeting? Bypass the email step completely and go right to the meaningful conversation.

Fifteen minutes on the phone can be the substitute for any back and forth emails. Save yourself significant time emailing back and forth, or worse, the multi-paragraph email, and pick up the phone. Get the summary of what you would have written (or read) and strengthen your relationship with the prospect at the same time. You can always send a follow-up email on the synopsis of what was discovered.

I was preparing to host a one-day event on sales skills and training specifically for Realtors and mortgage brokers. I have had a small following of this subset of people for a while and thought it was time to host an event specifically for them. I needed to fill the room and didn't have a lot of actual names, but plenty of connections on LinkedIn. I could have easily sent off an email blast to everyone on my list, and there is value in that. However, the connection, the reason why people should attend and the human factor would have been lost. I started finding people who fit the real estate professional demographic within my LinkedIn network. I then found their phone numbers and started calling. Yes, it took a lot of time and there were plenty of people who weren't interested, but after a week I was able to fill the room.

LinkedIn is a fabulous tool for finding out a ton about people. No other social media platform gives you access to a person's history, where they have lived, what city they live in now, hobbies and groups they volunteer with and their personal email and phone numbers.

One of the people I called on had been a Realtor for 35 years. I didn't know if he was the right fit, but maybe he had some younger Realtors working with him. I used the limited information I could find on his LinkedIn profile to start the conversation.

Hi, my name is Kim and we are connected on LinkedIn.

Hi, Kim. What can I do for you?

I noticed you've been in the real estate business for over three decades. That's super impressive. You've likely seen a lot of changes to the industry and business in Calgary in all that time.

Oh, yes. I've gone through several recessions, and because I take care of my team better than any of the other brokerages, I have been able to weather quite a few of the storms that have passed us.

And so on. This became a 30-minute conversation about how he'd grown his business, where he saw it going from there, and where he wanted to go next. Was he looking to retire? Did he have an exit strategy? Was he selling or passing on the business?

It turned out he was interested in doing more philanthropic tasks. He wanted to leave a legacy behind that was more than just his company's name. He wanted people to recognize the person behind the name.

Listen, the reason I wanted to call you was to invite you and any team members to an exclusive sales training event. We will be covering how the world of connection has changed and encourage those who are no longer comfortable getting on the phone how to do it effectively. We will be encouraging people to step out of their comfort zones and put human connection first and foremost. We will give everyone plenty of role play, exercise, and ultimately will leave people feeling pumped to create similar connections to what you and I did today in short amounts of time.

By the time I'd made my request for him to join our event, I knew a lot about him, his business, his priorities and where he saw his future. I asked a ton of questions, created a relationship, and from there, knew some of his key words and trigger points on what would appeal to him.

If you're not making phone calls, you're losing out on the opportunity to get to know people better.

You cannot be genuinely interested in helping people and helping their companies if you're not interested in having a true conversation with them.

Conversations like this cannot be done via email. You must make the call.

The Cost of a Call

How much is a call worth to you? This might seem like a silly question. But as it turns out, 78% of decision-makers have attended an event or purchased a product from a cold call. That means almost eight out of every 10 people you call on have said *yes* at some point. Imagine if every time they said *yes*, it was to you and not to someone else, or worse, your competitor.

Think about the product you sell, or maybe you sell different products and services. If you were to call someone for the first time, they said *yes* to meeting with you and that meeting eventually led to a sale, what is the value of that initial call?

I don't care if you are selling a product that is $1,000, $10,000 or $100,000+. If you knew every call was potentially a new client ready to say *yes* to someone, would you be making more calls? Chances are the answer would be yes.

So if you're not making the calls, you are leaving money on the table! People are saying *yes*, they're just not saying *yes* to you.

Why We're not Making the Call

Fear is too often the barrier standing in the way of most people making their first phone calls. People tell me they're afraid of what someone will say when they do pick up the phone. They are afraid of the person *not* picking up the phone. They are afraid of their response. They're afraid of the person on the other end being mean. And when I ask what would ultimately happen with all of this, fear takes over and leads to each person's worst nightmares.

Susan was afraid of making her first phone calls. She had crafted her message, and on paper it sounded all right, but until she said it out loud, she would never hear how it would actually sound.

"I can't," said Susan.

"What do you mean?" I asked.

"If I do call and they pick up, what if they slam the phone down on me?" she replied.

I usually smile at these types of fears because my answer is typically, "So what?" If that was to happen, would that even be a client you would ever want to work with? And if that did happen, how would it stop you from growing your business?

But the fear takes over and most people fall into the rabbit hole of despair, thinking that by being rejected over the phone, the person on the other line somehow has enough power to crush all your business-building dreams forever.

A lot of successful people have been rejected numerous times and they still became big. The fear will not kill you. Your business will survive. You are greater than all the fear in the world. And know for every bad thought there is a reasonable answer to get around it.

What if They're Mean?

I had a person tell me their biggest fear is they would call someone and the person on the other line would pick up and immediately start yelling on the phone. Imagine that! Think about yourself. Have you ever picked up a phone that was ringing and started yelling and swearing at the person *before* they even had a chance to talk? Probably not. And if you are someone who picks up your phone and greets the person on the other line with screams and cursing, chances are you have bigger issues than whatever the person on the other line is offering.

People are incredibly friendly over the phone, and oftentimes even if the person is calling and we're not interested, we will politely thank them for calling and say, "Thank you, but I'm not interested." Where's the fear in that?

When we think how someone may reject us over the phone, the idea of it is always far worse than the likely outcome. I have never received a phone call from someone offering me their products or services and my immediate response was to get uncontrollably angry, say I was going to call the cops, or threaten that I was going to hunt that person down. It all sounds really silly, doesn't it? And I don't think I have ever called anyone and that was their response. Yet most of us aren't making the call because of this unreasonable fear. So the next time you are stopping yourself from making the phone call because of this fear, really picture it. Picture how silly someone would look on the other end if they were receiving this phone call in the middle of a food court and they were turning red in the face screaming at someone who had just called them for the very first time. The vast majority of people are not like that. And if by chance you ever called someone like that you would never want to meet them in real life, anyway.

I'm Afraid of Being Rejected

We take rejection too personally. Someone may tell us they are not interested and we take that as if they are attacking our personality, our ethics or our family. It doesn't matter if you are working for someone else or your own company, being told, "I'm not interested," has nothing to do with who we are as people.

John Lydgate said, "You can't please all of the people all of the time." You're not going to have every single person you call completely agree to meet with you every time you call them. Timing is everything. And what may be a bad time today may be a great time six months from now.

But the fear of being rejected is so strong that instead of knowing we have to face and embrace rejection in order to get to where we want to be, some people would rather avoid the whole conversation altogether. This is why dating apps like Tinder have taken off. You don't know if the person rejects you, you only know if they approve of you.

When we put ourselves out there, we have the potential to gain so much more than the slight amount that we may possibly lose. But is it really losing if it was never ours to begin with?

The Irony is, we are rejected over the phone more than we realize. When people answer the call, unless they overtly say *not interested*, anything else we hear, we take positively, because that's what we *really* want to hear. We want to hear that the person would love to go forward, but they don't have the budget or they don't have the time or the best person to send information to is a generic inbox. The biggest rejection is "Send me some information," and for this we get excited.

There will always be people for whom our product or service isn't a perfect fit. And this is a good thing. If we had to sell to everyone, we would be overwhelmed with how this product fit everyone's needs. We want to spend our time on the people who *want* our products, not the ones who *need* it. We would spend a ton of time convincing someone our product will satisfy them, but unless they also want it, we could end up talking to a dead end.

A car salesperson may have someone walk into their dealership saying they need a car. There are plenty of vehicles which could satisfy this need. A car is really about having a mode of transportation that can get you conveniently from Point A to Point B. Let's assume this salesperson only sold minivans. For someone coming in who *wants* fashion and speed this will not be a fit. A minivan may serve the *needs* of the person—to get from Point A to Point B, but the person would never buy one if they *wanted* something different. The salesperson would end up wasting both her and the prospect's time because it's not addressing the *wants* of the buyer.

When someone tells us no for any reason, we take that as the ultimate end. Any time someone tells us no, they're not saying no forever, just no for now. In that particular moment in which you called, the prospect may not need your services—but life changes quickly, and that doesn't mean they never will.

A Realtor can approach a family and talk all about their services. If the family is happy with their current home and current neighborhood, it doesn't matter how good the Realtor is, how many families they've helped move or the amount the Realtor gets the seller above market price. If the time isn't right, someone isn't going to decide to sell their home *because* they met the perfect Realtor. So the Realtor sticks around. She follows up every few months or a year later, and suddenly the family is ready to sell. They are now empty nesters, the mother accepted a job transfer to a new city, there's a baby on the way, or a whole multitude of reasons why someone would suddenly need to sell their home when they weren't interested in Realtor services only a few months previously.

If the person is saying no to you, understand that circumstances can change and there will always be a reason to follow up. If they are saying no, they are not saying no to you, they are saying no to the opportunity, to their current circumstances and no to learning more. Tenacity will be your friend in this. Continue to follow up and you will be gifted with people who remember you and suddenly need your services.

It Feels Awkward

Of course it feels awkward! You are not practiced enough with it. Imagine someone sitting down in front of a piano the very first time. Would you expect them to play a Beethoven-composed piece? Of course you wouldn't. It takes time to get to that level. The first time I ever sat at a piano, I didn't know what the keys were. I didn't know how to read music. And if I banged on the keys, little less than noise came out. Over time,

I learned the fundamentals and started getting better every time I played.

Making calls is not much different. We're out of practice. We know how to phone someone close to us. I could easily spend an hour on the phone with my mother or my sisters. I could even call on someone I've had a few conversations with in the past. I talk about their pets, recent vacations and what is new with their business. But when I call someone for the first time, it can be difficult to know what to say.

Calling will feel the most awkward when we don't invite it to be a conversation. Making a phone call to someone is not about delivering a speech to a single audience member, it's about starting and continuing a relationship.

Public speaking is one of the biggest fears people have, and if the message we prepared is a little less than a three-minute speech, of course it's going to feel awkward. The person on the other end listens to your (prepared) ramble and they lose interest. That's not a great way to get positive reinforcement on which elements worked. Turn your initial call into a conversation and it will become more natural, more fluid and far less awkward.

Get Yourself Psyched!

I've heard many different ways people psych themselves up before making a call. Some people will listen to their favorite pumped-up song. Others will say out loud (and very loudly), "I can do this!" repeatedly as they dial the numbers. I encourage you to find something that works for you.

Even as you develop confidence on the phone, you will have that one call which will throw you off your game. You will find yourself in a slump where it feels as if no one wants to connect. And then it will feel nerve-racking to make that initial move again.

Prepare for that day. Know what you will do when that moment hits. Or if you'll need that extra jolt of enthusiasm. By being prepared when you don't need it, you will know what to do when you do need it.

I once ran a marathon. I joined a group of runners to help me with the marathon training. As we were getting closer to the race date, our coach told us to start mentally preparing for how we would get through "the wall," that moment when you feel like you have nothing left to give. When race day came, by the time I was three quarters into the run, I hit my wall. I wanted to stop. That's when I remembered what I'd mentally prepared for. I pictured my dog tied around my waist and she was pulling me to keep running. It was not the most inspiring thing, but in that moment it worked. I kept picturing my dog pulling me and my legs kept going until I found the energy again to focus on just the run itself.

Personally, when I find myself nervous to make a call to a person who is really high up on my goal list, I will remind myself, "Kim, people want to hear from you. You help companies connect with their clients on a deeper level and drive more revenue. Of course, the person on the other end wants to have a conversation about that." That will typically give me the reset I need to move past my own nervousness.

Your product, service, business and just you being you is bringing positive impact into this world. By not calling, by not telling them, you are doing a massive disservice to the world. Because most people don't know what they don't know. They need you to help them understand a way in which they can do so much more. You are a gift, and there are plenty of people who are already appreciative that you've entered their lives. Let's make that even more people. Go make the connection!

Chapter Ten

Why Questions

"**W**hat do I *say* to sell more?"

It was the question Derek asked me before I was about to go on stage at an event.

That question alone tells me everything I need.

Derek didn't have a thought-out sales process. He was layering previous clients example over example and giving his prospect all the answers previous prospects had asked him in the past. Derek thought he wasn't making the sales because he wasn't saying *enough*, when, in fact, he was talking too much and listening far too little.

And by trying to solve his problem by saying more, his struggle to sell was becoming worse.

When a prospect came to Derek for the first time, they didn't want to hear his index of every client he'd worked for.

They wanted to hear about what Derek was going to do for *them*. But Derek believed he would satisfy the prospect's desire to understand how they could work together by telling the prospect all the work he'd done for every company before them.

It's like meeting a date for the first time and they're explaining to you why they are relationship material because of all the amazing things they did for all the previous people they'd dated.

Gross.

No one wants to hear *more* about what you're capable of until they firstly agree you understand what they are looking for, what is stopping them from achieving their goals and *then* how your expertise will help them get there. Not because you did all this amazing stuff for all these other companies, but rather because you fully understand their problems and are able to solve them. That gives you the confidence to solve the prospect's challenges with the same method.

Sales is not about what we say. When we brag about our results with others early in the conversation, it may trigger immediate interest, but if we keep going, it will just lead to skeptical questions from the prospect. Those results may have worked for that person, or that business, or in that industry, or that geography...but that will never work for me.

As they hear one example after another, they'll start questioning, either internally or out loud. Will that really work for me? What if I get a different result (or no result)?

And then they'll (internally) list excuses about why it won't work for them.

When we ask questions and find out more about the prospect, we can better understand from the prospect's point of view what
3 they would love to see as their personal result. We want them to tell us what they picture. Why would it be different for them? What does their reality look like?

Only questions will pull out this information. Asking the right questions will help us to create a deeper connection with our prospect. Questions are inspired from genuine curiosity.

Anything we say to a prospect is up for skepticism. Anything a prospect tells us becomes truth.

When we ask powerful questions, we get powerful answers and create powerful conversations. Questions allow the other person to tell us what's most important to them.

Open-Ended vs. Closed-Ended Questions

There are two types of questions: open-ended questions and closed-ended questions.

If you ever took a journalism class or even a high school English class, the instructor probably instructed you to answer the *Six W's*: Who, What, Where, When, Why and How.

When a question is structured as an open-ended question, it forces the prospect to answer with a statement, whereas closed-ended questions force the prospect to answer with only a *yes* or *no*. Closed-ended questions will usually start with something similar to *are you, do you, have you* or *would you* but can cover a variety of different forms.

Throughout your sales conversations, you want to be asking a majority of your questions as open-ended questions. You will typically save your closed-ended questions for strategic moments when you need confirmation or are ready to close the deal.

The best way to know if a question is open-ended or closed-ended is to ask it to yourself. If the question can be answered with a simple *yes* or *no*, chances are you are asking a closed-ended question. Review your question and work on reframing it using a who, what, where, when, why or how at the beginning.

Until the prospect has provided us with the information we need to get the deal to cross over the finish line, asking closed-ended questions too early will put a lot of our own assumptions upon the prospect.

A perfect example of how asking the right type of question completely changed the conversation was when I was teaching a full-day sales training for a custom home builder.

One of the salespeople was performing a role play on her sales conversation with a pretend prospect. Her questions went something like this:

Is this your first time buying a custom home?
Will your husband be involved in the decision?
Are you looking to move in within the year or sometime later?

Almost all her questions continued down this path, and after a couple more questions, I stopped her.

Her questioning process was forcing many assumptions and decisions on her pretend prospect that didn't need to be there and therefore forced her prospect to agree to things which may not be entirely accurate.

I invited her to consider how much different the conversation would be if each one of those questions were turned open-ended.

What a difference in how the conversation would evolve. With just a slight reframing of the questions, the home seller would ask:

What is your custom home buying experience?
Who else would need to be involved in the decision?
When would you ideally like to move in?

In the first question, yes, it might be the first time the home buyer is building a custom home, but does that mean they've had *no* experience with buying a custom home? The new question now opens up the conversation to the experience their sister, cousin, neighbor or co-worker had. The prospect may talk about the conversations they've had with other people in order to narrow down this particular homebuilder as part of the decision-making process.

Before, when the home seller asked, "Will your husband be a part of this decision?" they were likely wanting a *yes* answer so she might insist that the next meeting involves the husband in the design and experience. However, with the second question, "Who else would need to be involved in this decision?" can now open up the conversation that the home buyer wants to involve her children in the decision. Perhaps they want to create a suite for an aging parent and they want that parent to have a say in the design of that suite. There may be more people involved in the decision now, but that doesn't have to be a negative. With more people involved, there is more opportunity to get each of the individuals emotionally excited about the soon-to-be home building process. As a parent, I know when my children are excited, it's hard to say *no* to anything that brings them joy.

Finally, the last question was the most assumptive. As the home seller, they are doing their best to lead the conversation so the home buyer chooses a date this year. However, now the home buyer not only has to give you a timeframe but will also typically justify the reason they chose that date.

The home buyer may have every intention of moving in this year, but that could mean a lot of different things to different people. Maybe the home buyer wants to move in, in September. Why? Because the kids will be starting at a new school and the new home will mean less commuting time for the family. Maybe the home buyer dreams of hosting Christmas dinner in their new home and wants to ensure they are moved in by mid-November at the latest.

There are lots of dates the home buyer might provide, and as the seller, it's up to you to ask the right questions and then continue to dig deeper.

And as a bonus, whenever I get a satisfactory answer from a client, I love throwing in, "Why is that important?" at the end. It pushes the prospect to give you an even more specific and meaningful answer.

Closed-Ended Questions Posing as Open-Ended Questions

When students start to become more aware of their questions, they start by doing better with the *Six W* questions, but then they will begin to revert to a hybrid of closed-ended questions trying to pose as open-ended questions.

There are two versions of the closed-ended posing as open-ended questions: you still get the *yes/no* response, or now you are getting a single-word response.

Taking the earlier example of the custom home builder, one of the questions the salesperson asked in her pretend client meeting was, *What room is most important to you?*

In this case, because she was specifically asking for a single word answer, it was a closed-ended question.

Another version of this is one of my absolute most hated questions in the world: *What is your budget?*

I'll go further into how to better reframe that question in the next chapter, but the reason I hate that question is the seller is looking for a specific number, whereas the client will typically give the standard response: There is no budget.

Typically, closed-ended questions are when people try to focus on the open-ended part of a question and without realizing it preface it with a closed-ended question.

Questions such as:
Is this HOW you would like to see it?
Is this WHAT you would want to do?
Are you WHERE you want to be?
Do you know WHY you would like it that way?
Is there anyone else WHO would need to be engaged?
WHAT if I could show you...would that work for you?

Spend time planning and writing out your questions before every meeting. As you write them out, see if you can answer them with a direct *yes* or *no* answer. If you can, do your best to reframe them. If you can't, then you're doing great.

Feel welcome to pull out that list when you are meeting with your prospect in a sales meeting. Most people shudder when they hear me recommend pulling out a list of questions. They fear that by doing so, it will make them look amateur. On the contrary. Pulling out a list of prepared and well-thought-out questions actually makes you look prepared.

Hands down, if I was in a sales meeting and the person who was sitting across from me was trying to sell me their services and they pulled out a list of questions they wanted to ask me, I would be astounded. This person knows what they want, has the intention set in place and is ready to ask the right questions to get us both there with full respect for my time.

Less is More

As you start to form your questions, it can be easy to create a lengthy preface to the question. We will sometimes feel like we need to justify the question before we ask it. I've heard people talk about the clients they work with, their business or the way they've helped others first. There can be as many as two or three sentences before getting to the question.

Stop it!

You don't need to introduce your question before asking it. If the client doesn't understand the question, then re-frame it and ask it in another way. If they still don't understand the question, go ahead and create a leading statement to help them get to the answer.

Oftentimes, I will sit quietly for a moment before trying to explain further. What I am hoping to do is see where their thought patterns started the moment they heard the question.

One of the questions which will typically always get a follow-up question for more clarification will be when I ask, "What do you want to achieve by this time next year?"

Sometimes people will answer right off the bat.

Other times, the person who has received the question will ask, "What do you mean? Financially? Otherwise?"

That's when I will typically smile and respond with, "Everything that came to mind."

Yes, I want to hear their financial goals, because they are measurable and are a good way of reverse-engineering how to get to that goal. But I am also interested in the other goals they have for themselves, the ones which may not be quantifiable or they are not easily able to create the tasks which will better get them there.

If I clarify the question too soon, I may have a creative person tell me all about their financial obligations and why they need to hit certain revenue numbers. For many creative people, thinking logically will move them out of their creative space and it will be difficult to hear the other, more important reasons to them on why they want to achieve certain levels of success.

If anything, instead of trying so hard for your prospect to understand your question, provide space for the client to provide an answer that is authentic to them. Discover the prospect's truth first, before diving in and trying to get the prospect to understand what you need to hear.

Creating a Conversation-Starting Message

When I first started in sales, the management team would drill into us what our elevator pitch would be. The elevator pitch was one of the most important phrases a salesperson back then had to memorize, because it briefly described what we sold in a way that could be delivered if the CEO was waiting at the elevator bank with you and you were riding up the elevator to the top floor. It had to be less than 30 seconds and ideally be enough to get you a meeting.

The elevator pitch has significantly evolved since that time. A great book to read that covers this topic further is Daniel Pink's *To Sell Is Human*. He makes some great arguments on how the elevator pitch has truly evolved into not a standard statement, but a selection of several different ones.

There is a lot to be said for creating a version of each of Pink's different elevator pitches. If there is only one that should take over your elevator pitch entirely, that would be asking a question.

Throughout the entire **KO Sales** cycle, the common theme is to ask more powerful questions to get more powerful answers. Questions incite conversations. And what better way to create a conversation when you are on a phone call the very first time with a new prospect than to ask the person on the other line a question?

Oftentimes we need to be clear about our value proposition before creating the question.

The fastest way to determine the value you provide a client is to ask yourself--what does the client *ultimately* get when they are <u>finished</u> experiencing your service?

Whatever that answer is, turn it into an open-ended question which can be posed to the client to help incite conversation.

For instance, when I teach someone sales strategy they ultimately get:

Better cash flow predictability

Faster deal closes

Higher revenue per client

A question I could ask the person would be: *How would better cash flow predictability help your company to expand?*

Or perhaps: *What more could your company accomplish if the deals you were working on closed faster and for more revenue?*

These now become conversation starters, not throwing information at the prospect and hoping there is enough there to make the other person want to ask *us* questions.

Chapter Eleven

Lead Qualification
and the Power of BANT

Before going too far into the sales cycle and buyer's journey, we want to make sure the prospect we are working with is properly lead-qualified. We want to ensure the person with whom we are continuing to work and the goals they have--and the solution to help them get there faster--is something they want to address within a fairly urgent timeframe.

Lead qualification happens early and often throughout the sales process, because things can change.

I can't tell you the number of times I've been in the middle of a sales cycle, we would have several meetings and then I would start my meeting the way I always do with, "What has changed since the last time we met?" Suddenly, the answer would be that an important person involved in the decision-making process has left their role, budgets were suddenly a constraint, a new supplier came in a showed them a different solution and they wonder if it will work better for them, and so on.

One time I was working for American Express and I worked very hard to get the initial meeting with a very large national grocery chain. We were looking at a solution that could potentially save them millions of dollars a year and help them improve their cash flow situation significantly (which is a very big thing in the grocery industry. Deliveries of food are made and expected to be paid almost immediately). We had several meetings, did hours of analysis, presented the proposal and were now ready to sign the agreement. Because of the significance of the size of the contract and the massive change the company would have to undergo to work with us, our contract had to go through a process called *red-lining* where both companies' teams of lawyers would review the contract and make, and agree or disagree to, changes to the terms.

I arrived at my meeting time. I called my manager to hang on standby because he should expect a very excited call in a bit more than an hour, and I walked into the client's building.

When I met the gentleman who was going to sign the contract, we had some light small talk and then I asked the same question I asked at every meeting. "Has anything changed since the last time we met?"

This time he said something had.

Not the thing you want to hear when you are about to sign an agreement. I took a deep breath and hoped for the best.

Maybe they needed the solution sooner. Maybe they needed access to more American Express credit.

Then my point of contact told me, "We've been purchased by another company. Everything is frozen."

Unfortunately, I didn't get the deal. The parent company was owned by one of my counterparts in the east and nothing more could be done.

But if I would have tried to push forward without asking the question, how long would he have nicely allowed me to walk through the contract? Would he have eventually said *no* without an explanation? And in the event it was something smaller and less significant than being bought out, would I have been able to talk through and still save the deal if I didn't know what I was dealing with?

Lead qualification happens at the initial engagement with the client. We don't want to spend more time than is necessary if the client is not an ideal fit for us.

There are a few areas we will qualify for. If we don't have the answers to any one of them then we don't have a sales cycle.

I like using the acronym BANT to complete lead qualification. Now, there are lots of opinions out there on whether BANT is still relevant or not. I've seen plenty of other acronyms out there which include other areas of questioning that we will cover later in this book. But for the lead qualification stage, BANT is really all you need. And sometimes, simpler is better.

BANT was developed by IBM several decades ago and became the primary questioning area for them, and now for us.

The BANT acronym stands for the areas we need to question for: Budget, Authority, Need and Timeline. BANT is the checklist of the areas that are qualified and understood. BANT is not the order of the questions we ask.

It likely doesn't make sense to meet a client for the first time and try to run through BANT in the order the acronym is listed. Imagine starting a conversation by asking about the prospect's budget without understanding the need or timeline. That may come across as abrasive and could become a quick way of ending a sales cycle before it really ever gets off the ground.

The rest of the chapter will cover how we question in each of these areas and what we are ultimately seeking through the questioning process.

Budget

Budget is one of the first things we need to know within a sales cycle and one of the last things we need to discover in the lead qualification process. As much as we'd like to ask the client about it first, it's not the nicest way to start a relationship. It's like asking your date, "How much do you make?" before the server has even taken your drink order. Chances are, your date will be nice enough to stick around, but there won't be a second date.

One of the absolute worst questions you can ask your client is, "How much do you have allocated for this project?" Yes, you're getting right to the point. But whether the client has money set aside or doesn't, the answer will be *nothing* or something far less than you expected. Don't get caught in this trap! The client honestly believes they don't have anything to spend on this project, or far less than they are willing to dedicate. It is your job as the high-value service provider to help the client see the impact of their investment first--before determining how much they are willing to invest.

A budget tells us what we can't afford, but it doesn't stop us from buying it.

Buying a Website

When I was last shopping around for a new website, I went around to my network and asked who would be best-suited to provide this. I had three different acquaintances come back to me.

The first woman said she would love to do my project. She asked me to fill out a Google Form with everything that I was looking for. Was it WordPress? Custom design? Would I have to transfer over blogs and other files? Do I need copy created or would I do that myself?

The entire form took about 20 or 30 minutes to fill out. Asking for tons of details, things I thought I knew and things I had no idea, such as: name some websites you currently like and would like to replicate. I wish I had known that. It was one of those things where I would see a website for the first time and fall in love with it and then completely forget all about it. I had no idea where to start with that answer.

At the end of the form, it asked the burning question: "What is your investment for this project?" Nicely worded. But yet again, I had no idea. The last website I had created was my first professionally-done website, which was created on a startups budget. It was a simple WordPress design and cost me $1,500. It was good, I just outgrew it. How much more was I willing to spend? I had no idea. I thought about it reasonably and with the expectation that whatever number I wrote in that question might or might not come back to haunt me. Put a number too high and I might end up with an over-complicated website that I spent way too much on. Put too little and I might be told I am out of my mind. It wasn't like I was shopping around for websites on a regular basis. I had no idea even where to begin. So I put $5,000. That seemed reasonable. If my first investment lasted me three years, this should easily get me another three more years and hopefully not break before that period of time.

The woman called me the next day and we booked a time to walk through what a standard $5,000 website would look like and how it would function. Fair enough, I thought to myself. I don't think I really need more than that. After all,

I'm not a major organization. I don't need internal logins and customer portals. I just need to communicate my message.

The second person called me up. He was really excited to meet with me. When we last ran into each other at a local conference I was telling him how I was strongly poised to finally hit that elusive $1M revenue mark. Maybe not exactly hit it, but with my third year of business I was DETERMINED to make my first $83,000 month, and if I could do that once, I could do it again and again, which ultimately makes me a $1M company.

He was thrilled. "We need to meet," he insisted.

We booked a time to sit down later the following week. I came into his office and he gave me a 20-minute presentation about his company, the companies he collaborates with, and the projects they have completed. The full 20-minutes was spent talking about his company and how the very best companies choose to work with him and his outsourced team.

Later that week, I received a proposal from him. The email contained a very pretty pdf document reiterating why so many companies go with him. He even included a personalized video of him telling me how he was excited to be my partner on this project. When I saw the price tag I laughed, I was so shocked. I honestly thought there was an error at first, but nope, it was there. $72,000. For a website. For *my* website.

Now I'm not saying that $72,000 is a huge number for a website. It may not be. Everything is relative. If my company was generating millions at that time it might have made a lot of sense. We just weren't there yet.

Then I started to really analyze his entire proposal. At a $72,000 price point, I would fully expect the proposal to be flawless. I started to cut it up in my head. There was a spelling error. The video had terrible shadowing and looked as if it had been filmed on a cell phone. I would expect that a company asking for a premium price would deliver nothing less than perfection, from proposal stage to final delivery. I thought to myself if the proposal is weak and anything less than perfect, what would they consider acceptable for my website?

When he called me a couple of days later after not hearing anything back from me, I asked him, "Why is the proposal so expensive?" He replied, "You said you wanted the best. The best costs that much."

Hmmm.

The third company I considered working with asked if we could sit down for a meeting. Sure. At this point I had nothing to lose.

We spent the entire first meeting trying to figure out of what I would want my website to be a reflection. We talked about how websites are like an online business card. What is the first impression I wanted someone to know about me? What do I offer? What action would I want someone to take? Who is my ideal audience? How would my ideal client know they are in the right place when they came to my website? And so on.

We agreed to meet for a second time, and this time around they talked about the advantages of a WordPress site and custom-built websites. Each possible solution had its unique challenges and strengths. But we weren't talking about a specific solution just yet. We were collaborating on what would be the best solution for me and my business outside of their company providing that solution. It felt like a safe zone. I was honest and open and transparent, and so were they, throughout the entire process.

During our third meeting, we started to walk through a proposal. I had a lot of questions and I was grateful to have someone there to answer them.

On the fourth meeting, I signed the deal--for five times more than I had told the first woman what my budget was in her Google Form.

Budget is just one aspect of the conversation and there is always value in what we create with our clients. When we create the value of the conversation first, the right amount of investment will come as a result of what we are *creating* for our clients, not what they are willing to pay.

Understanding the Big Goal First

When I worked for American Express, we often had to deal with a company's procurement department. The manager of procurement was often mandated with one task: save 2% of operating spend.

Most vendors would hear that and immediately rebid with the procurement person with a price that was 2% less than what the client had been paying the year before. They become so afraid of losing the deal that they would rather comply with the request than to spend a bit of extra time challenging the status quo.

I, however, would go in and start digging into the other areas of the business that I knew my product and service would affect. When I heard the procurement manager needed to reduce spend by 2% of operating spend, I would hear that as *all* operating spend. That didn't mean just my product line.

Often, we would take some time to dig into the other areas in which they were spending and find out the manager was spending on software or processes that would become redundant with a greater investment with my company, for less than what they would spend on each individual piece. The elimination of one expense and a slight increase in another area would be more overall savings than the investment I would then typically ask the person to make with me and my company.

When we think about the budget, it's not about how much we want the client to spend, but what their ultimate goal is for their role, their department or the organization as a whole.

Most companies' desire isn't just to *save* money, but rather *make* money. They want to grow, expand and attract new markets. It's far easier to get a person to picture where they want to be and what that would look like than to try to help them avoid what they fear. The only time a company's goal will be to save more money is when they can't picture being able to make more revenue, so then they focus on profitability (and reducing expenses), and then finally just eliminate all expenses. Keep the client focused on the bigger vision. They will be more excited to invest when the image is to invest to help them grow.

When we approach the conversation with what the client's goals are first and foremost, that becomes the primary conversation. Then our service becomes one aspect to help them get there.

When someone has a goal of losing 10 pounds, there are plenty of ways they can get there, and sometimes they have to do many things in order to get there. Someone may start to change their eating habits, look at cardio and incorporate weight training. You might claim one will help all achieve that goal the fastest, but it's better to look at this realistically and admit you will need multiple avenues to get you there sustainably, and it's good to test what is best for each individual. If you were selling training, cardio could mean running, spin class, swimming, rowing or even jumping rope. But just asking a client what training they want to take is no different than asking a client what their budget is. The client is usually open to possibilities, they just want to feel secure in knowing their goal will be met quickly and easily. It's less about the specific *how* and more about the big goal.

Budget Questions

With the budget, our goal is to ask questions that will lead us to a financial conversation. This does not have to be how much the client has to spend, but rather how much do they believe they will *make*. People love talking about their goals and where they hope to be. Your job as the seller will be to understand what the client reasonably believes is their growth potential and the impact any improvement in their business will have on their overall financial situation.

Unless we are confirming what we already know, questions in the lead qualification stage should all be open-ended questions.

What are your goals within the next six months? One year? Two years? (Rarely do I ask what the goals are longer than that because for most businesses, a five-year goal is more of a guiding light then a path set in stone. I also want them to see this as an immediate resolution to their immediate needs. We also need to drive them to a *quantifiable* goal. Answers such as "becoming the market leader" is meaningless if we don't know how much we need to sell to get there. Becoming nationally recognized is meaningless if we don't know how to measure that achievement.)

What would it mean to you to have _____? (This is the *impact* your service or product will provide someone. For instance, when we sell sales training, we ask about a proper sales process, predictable cash flow, a strategy to sell more services in a predictable time frame...)

How many more clients/more revenue/more profitability will that bring you?

Once we understand what the dollar value of their goal is, it is easier to position ourselves as a portion of that revenue growth.

We can easily position a $20,000 product to a company whose goal is to achieve an extra $200,000 profit before the end of this year. It may be a lot more difficult to position the same product to a company who wants to achieve an extra $50,000 profit this year. But in both scenarios, if we would have asked the standard, "What's your budget?" question, the answer likely would have been, "Nothing."

Authority

There are often many people involved in every business decision, even for small businesses. With larger companies and sales cycles, you may never deal directly with the decisionmaker or the final-approval person. That is perfectly okay. What's not okay is not knowing who that person is and how they will make their final decision or impact the recommendation in the decision-making process.

By understanding the authority or decision-making process, it will help us to navigate the sales journey for our next steps and future meetings.

Influencer and Decisionmaker

Oftentimes there are two main people involved in the sales process from the client's side: the influencer and the decisionmaker. In much larger companies, where you may have to work with eight or 12 individuals throughout the process, you may run into other roles, such as neutral parties, adversaries, technicians and various other roles. However, those roles become less important when as a seller we stay goal-oriented with your prospect right from the beginning.

The influencer is often the person who gathers the information. They may recommend to the decisionmaker which direction to take, whereas the decisionmaker will be the person who ultimately makes the decision to go forward or not.

If the lead comes from an inbound source, such as they contacted you from a *contact us* form or submitted information through some call-to-action (CTA), they could be either the influencer or the decisionmaker. When we are reaching out cold for the first time, the goal is to always ask for the decisionmaker the first time.

How do you know who is the decisionmaker? I like to say the person who will sign the contract will usually be the person who has final say on the project.

Many times through the sales cycles, you may end up dealing almost entirely with the influencer, with the decisionmaker coming in near or right at the end, if at all. It's okay to only be dealing with the influencer. What's not okay is know how that chain of command works.

If you decide ignorance is bliss in your sales cycle, you are setting yourself up for massive failures. The last place you ever want to be is where you have met with your client several times. You believe the solution is defined and they seem to be agreeable about the investment, and then right as you're about to sign the contract they say to you, "This looks good. I just need to run it by Sally." You immediately think to yourself, "Who in the *world* is *Sally*?!"

Even when we know we are dealing with the decisionmaker, we need to know who else will be involved in the decision.

In my company, I am the ultimate decisionmaker. I am the president of my organization and I am the ultimate sayer of yea or nay. However, I have a team of people. We have instilled a strong *owner mentality* with many members of the team and I would never make a hiring decision until having everyone on the team be a part of the vetting process. I would never make a large financial decision without hearing everyone's opinion on the investment. Sometimes I even run ideas past my husband.

If someone was trying to sell to me and didn't understand who else was going to be a part of the decision, that's when we run into situations where I could be, "Go, go, go...whoa..."

Get to know all the players who will have an influence in every decision and ensure you are asking the right questions to ensure you are setting yourself up for success.

Decision-Making Process

With each person in the decision-making process, they each have their own primary criteria on how they will make a decision. Different roles and personalities will have different components of a decision as most important to them. Some roles, usually in the operation or technician type roles, will insist on the cost factor, whereas roles which are visionary and strategic will want to see the impact it places on their organization and people.

When we are creating something amazing for a client, we want to work with the strategic and visionary roles. They are the dreamers and have more willingness to take the risks to get to the next level. We want to ask how they will determine the right solution for them and how do they rank various criteria with which they will be selecting a winning vendor.

Authority Questions

We want to ask questions that will both help us determine the chain of command in the decision-making process and how that decision will be made. In the event you are not going to be dealing with the decisionmaker (or not until much later in the sales process), this is where we also ensure we understand what will is important to those others in the organization and how they will be determining their decision.

Once again, we want to avoid closed-ended questions. Just like when you were told to avoid the question, "What's your budget?" it will result in the single word answer that may not be accurate. Asking the closed-ended questions, "Are you the decisionmaker?" or, "Is there anyone else involved?" will result in an answer that will limit the conversation to only the person you are currently dealing with. Of course, the person you're talking to is the decision maker, or at least they're the only person that matters at this stage of the game, and there isn't anyone else involved. Then you'll spend all your time working with the "the only person" involved in this decision-- that is, until they're not, because it's time to sign the contract.

Some influencers don't want to feel their power is being taken away when we ask if they are the decisionmaker, so they say they are. Beware. Buyers can be liars. Ask the right open-ended questions and we expand the conversation, not limit it.

Once we know who else will be a part of this decision, we next want to know how the decision to choose you as the right solution provider will be determined.

We want to encourage the client to tell you that price is not their number one criteria when making a decision. If they are insistent on the price, now's the time to walk away. As a high-value service provider, you shouldn't pride yourself on the lowest price. That's a fast way to the bottom.

What we do want to hear is the prospect is looking for high quality, service capabilities, long-term relationships, single-service provider that can meet multiple needs, a single company that can help them to save *overall,* or over the lifetime of their relationship, not just in one specific area, and so on. Know what differentiates you and help your prospect to say that's what they are looking for. If the prospect doesn't answer naturally, you can use leading questions, which will be covered in the chapter Leading Questions.

Questions you can ask to determine the decision-making hierarchy and understand how the decision will be made:

Who else will be involved in this decision?
What is most important for that person to see?
What is most important to you in any solution you find?
How will you determine this is the right solution for you?
When will we be involving others in the information discovery?

You'll notice the open-ended question, "Who else will be involved in this decision?" opens up the conversation much more. We're not assuming the person we are speaking with is not the decisionmaker. On the contrary. This question can be posed just as easily to the decisionmaker as the influencer, or anyone else in the organization. It invites the response about who may have an active part or background role in the sales process.

Need

Why does the prospect need to change? What will they gain by taking on any new project?

Understanding the Need is usually one of the first areas that we will lead qualify a prospect on. It is the most important, because without a need to change, why are you here?

There are several things that we test to see if the prospect is ready to change. The first is, do they *want* to change. This may seem like a silly question, but it's important. A doctor can't help an obese person lose weight if they have no desire to change their way of life. A financial manager can't help someone save and invest if they don't want to stop spending their money on eating out and new clothes. And you as a seller can't help someone better their lives if they don't want to change the things they are doing.

And this may not just be up to the decisionmaker to decide. It may be also up to the person who will have to make the change every day. For instance, Sally the receptionist may be responsible for doing all the invoicing and payment reconciliation at your prospect's location. You have a brand-new software which can streamline the process, making invoicing only a couple of button clicks and automatically taking care of payment reconciliation. However, if Sally is set in her ways, has no desire to learn anything new and the prospect isn't willing to push that button, it doesn't matter how great your software is. There is no desire to change.

Yes, we will help our clients make their lives better. And yes, our service or product may save hundreds or thousands of hours, dollars and frustrations. But as the old saying goes, you can lead the horse to water, but you can't make him drink.

Don't waste your time with those who *need* your services but don't *want* your services. It will be a battle you will never win.

Need Questions

Most of the time, if the lead comes through an inbound source (they found you online, they searched out your solution or product, they asked around for a solution and you were referred), this is an easy conversation. The prospect recognizes there is a better way of completing a current process. They are looking to improve.

If you have a strong outbound sales game (and I highly recommend you create one), most of the prospects you encounter the first time will likely not know they need your services at that time.

The first questions we ask the prospect are very narrow and specific in the beginning and then open up to expand the opportunity after we know the prospect may become one of our ideal clients.

Like our opening question when calling or email a prospect, we want to very quickly clarify the *impact* our product and service will provide a business, without going into too much of what we do or how we do it. We save those conversations for much later in the sales process.

Then, once the prospect is open to having more conversations, we want to know the *impact* any change we implement on an individual or business will have on the greater picture. We want to create a bigger impact with the client. We want their current state to get to a point that they can't take it anymore, even if, up until we met them, everything was fine. We want them to see the world can be so much brighter when they work with us.

Questions in this area can also take on a variety of forms. We don't have to ask simple open-ended questions, although the vast majority of questions will be. We can also ask scaling questions (from 1-10) and comparison questions (who else in your industry?).

What would be the benefit to your company if [impact] occurred? (Where [impact] is the ultimate result of doing business with you. For example, when I sell sales training, sales training is not the impact, but rather cash flow predictability, more confidence meeting with prospects, being able to close deals faster, and so on. I would pick only one per question as opposed to stacking them together.)

Where do you want to be in the next six months or one year? (This is different than the budget question because with the budget question I am looking for a financial response. In this question I am looking for a purposeful response. The question can be asked just once, and then invite the client to provide you more depth to their response.)

Why is that important? (Always a favorite, and classic question. Make this part of your regular questioning.)

What would this allow you to do?

How are you currently managing?

What would your ideal state look (or feel) like?

How would you know you achieved that?

On a scale from 1-10, how ready are you to make this change?

To whom in your industry do you compare yourself and why?

You can see from the questioning, the Need portion of BANT can get very deep and heavy very fast. This is good. Depending on the length of your sales cycle (which is mostly determined by the investment the client has to put forward for your product or service), you may be in Need for an entire meeting or two.

Once the client has agreed there is both a need to change and a willingness to do so, you'll find that most of your Need questions will start to overlap with your value-creation questions, which will be covered in a later chapter.

Timeline

Although we want to ensure every area is BANT is covered, for me, timeline is one of the most critical areas we will explore. And it's not about getting a date, it's about figuring out *why* that date is important to the client.

When testing for timeline, this is where most people will typically ask what I consider to be *terrible* questions. Questions such as, "When do you want to start?" or, "When do you want to make your decision by"?

When I worked for Xerox, our standard question was, "By when do you want to make your decision?" As if somehow knowing when someone wanted to make a decision would make the sale cycle move faster.

There were often a lot of factors in play, including the client admitting they *need* a new copier. But surprise, surprise, even when they provided a date on when the decision needed to be made, it wasn't as if we could hold the client accountable for the date. The decision date was picked arbitrarily. Or another common answer would be, "As soon as possible." Even when someone asks me when I want to make a decision, whether it's for hiring my next employee or hiring their agency to help me build my business, my answer is usually, "Yesterday." For me, I want my decisions already made, but it doesn't mean I've found the right fit for my company, and that's why I'm still on the hunt.

The only reason our clients want to make their decisions "as soon as possible" is so they can focus on the areas of their business which are more important than evaluating vendor fits, negotiating terms and assigning resources to help implement the solution. They don't want to be spending more time making this decision--and definitely not with this terrible salesperson who is reminding them they still need to spend more time making a decision.

When do You want to be Finished?

The decision for a timeline is not about when the client wants to get started but rather *when* they want to be finished with their decision. When do they want to see the project complete? Ideally, as wonderful a person as you are, the client doesn't want to know what it's going to be like working with you. What they really care about is when you've finished your project and now they get to experience a better life without you there. Sorry, heart-centered people. You've made your client's lives better, they just don't want to have to rely on you any further.

I was teaching sales to a luxury custom home builder and the question about timeline came up. When I asked the team what they typically asked to test the prospect on their timeline, I received the same type of questions. "When would you like to start your home building process?"

I explained the question was absolutely terrible because without the context of understanding how long it takes to pick out designs, build, do site checks and eventually move in, the question is almost rhetorical. The prospect might choose any date, but it doesn't tell the home purchaser what they are ultimately interested in: living in the home.

If I have never built a luxury custom home before, do I choose a date six weeks from when I want to move in or six months, or do I just say "as soon as possible" without having secured all the right financing with my bank first?

By changing the questions with the client on the end destination, it makes it easier for them to picture the result. "When would you like to be moved into your new home?" Now the client has a question they can understand and answer.

Choosing to start the process is only the beginning of a long journey. We want to client to be focused on the final result. If you wanted to lose weight, would you want to be asked, "When do you want to start your gym membership?" The answer is usually right away, or yesterday, or six months ago. But none of that means they are going to be consistent with their gym schedule or be willing to invest in additional classes or personal training services. We put the focus on getting the gym membership, not the result the person is hoping to achieve by going to the gym. However, when we ask, "When would you like to have the dream body you imagine?" we're now putting focus on the idea that we have completed our journey (at least for now).

The goal with understanding the client's timeline is to get a *date*.

By focusing on an actual date and not some arbitrary timeline, we now can work backward with our client on the steps that need to be taken so the prospect will receive the full result he or she imagines.

If I asked someone when they want to see their sales volume increase from our sales program and the response back from the prospect was, "Sometime next quarter," that's a large window to work with. Our sales program is a 10-week program, so the answer sometime next quarter--does that mean they want to begin right away and start seeing the results within the quarter or does that mean they want to start engaging three months from now?

Yet I see too many business owners and sales professionals accept that as a response from their prospects.

Get the prospect to clarify the date as much as possible so you *both* have an end game toward which to work.

To ensure the date wasn't arbitrarily picked from the sky, the next step is then to understand *why* that date is important.

Why is that Important?

When we understand *why* a date is important for a client, it helps us to strengthen the entire sales cycle and move things forward quickly in the event decisions get stalled.

The date is less important than the *why*. Dates shouldn't be picked at random and rather should be somehow tied into another area of their business or life.

A client needs to be moved into their new home by September because that's when their kids will be starting at their new school.

A business needs to have their new accounting software up, running and staff fully trained by January 1 because that is their new fiscal year and they want to have clean accounting records from only one software.

A company needs to have sales training completed by the end of May because when they hit their seasonally-slow period, they now have the skills to start more prospect conversations, ultimately setting themselves up for revenue success for their third quarter and allowing them to invest in new geographies and grow their business 50% year after year.

With each one of those examples, there was a date. The date was now tied to when the client would be *completed* with the product or service, and there was a strong *why* attached to it.

The stronger the *why*, the greater the chance you will be able to continue to push the client to close. Because now the client is no longer just making a decision based on the product or service you deliver, but on the impact that decision will have on their overall business and lives.

If you feel the answer the client is giving you is weak when you ask, "And why is that date important?" continue asking again and again until you see what the impact is.

Client: We need sales training.

Me: Our sales training is 10-weeks of content over 12 weeks. When would you like to be completed?

Client: I suppose if we started right away we would be finished at the end of May.

Me: And why is May an important date for you? What would you be able to do?

Client: We would be going into our slower season better prepared. Maybe we could turn this ship around and it doesn't have to be our slow season.

Me: And why would not having a slow season be important?

Client: Then we can have a really strong Q3. We would like to hit the growth numbers we were doing only a couple of years ago, which was 50% year-over-year.

Me: And why is hitting 50% year-over-year important?

Client: Because then we can really expand our offering into new geographies and grow significantly.

You can see the answers I am ultimately seeking don't just happen with a single question and response. In this example, I had to ask, "Why is that important?" three times before I was satisfied with the strong answer the client gave me.

When we don't push to understand the reasoning behind a date, we can end up leaving the important information that will eventually help us to push the sales cycle forward.

When Stephanie met with her client to discuss a new app she'd created, she asked the question, "When do you want to see this app fully functional?" They responded with, "By the end of next quarter." Unfortunately Stephanie left it there.

By not taking the questioning to the next step, the client arbitrarily picked, "By the end of next quarter." What's stopping them from delaying the project another quarter? And why is that date that so important?

We continue to ask, "Why is that important?" until we eventually tie in the date to something that is either emotionally motivating to the client, or in the case of many businesses, until we tie it into a revenue or profit initiative.

When Stephanie went back to the client to ask them *why* the end of the next quarter was important for them to have the project completed, the client responded that they were going to be launching a new marketing campaign promoting the app.

"And *why* is that important?" Stephanie asked further.

"Because it will allow us to get as many downloads as possible and ultimately be able to push out our new lower-priced monthly subscription," the client responded.

"And how much revenue are you projecting that to bring in for your business?" Stephanie continued.

"We expect it to bring in an extra $100,000 a month."

Ahhh… now we have something.

Now that Stephanie was tying her project to the potential of the client bringing in an extra $100,000 per month, do you think they are more motivated to keep the project on track?

You could argue that the client likely knows the reasoning why they chose that date to begin with, so it becomes irrelevant for Stephanie to continue questioning. But you would be surprised by how many clients actually don't know. They will choose a date, and until they are questioned all the way through the reasoning behind their decision, the client may not have made the full connection.

Timeline Questions

With timeline questions, remember to focus on the end goal, the reasons *why* and ultimately drive to a date from the client.

By when would you like to see this completed?

What specific date would you like to set as the target?

Why is that important?

When this is completed, what will this allow your company to achieve/allow you to be?

What milestones will be important for you?

What else will your company be capable of once this project is complete?

Chapter Twelve

Powerful Questions Lead to Powerful Answers

As the sales cycle continues to move forward, the questions become more and more powerful. We want to continue to understand more about our clients, their goals, and more importantly--*why is that important* to them?

The more questions we ask, the more we get to uncover about our clients desires and how our service will help them.

Because sales is never about what we tell the client. It's about the questions we ask.

The person who asks the questions owns the conversation.

When a client starts peppering us with questions, such as:
What does it cost?
When can it be delivered?
Who else have you done work for?

How will you prove your return on investment?

Who owns that conversation? The client. They want you to answer in a way that is somehow going to convince them you are the best service offering.

When we spin the conversation around and are the ones to *ask* all the questions, we now have the opportunity to lead the client to the answers they need to hear--because they tell themselves what they need to hear.

Asking Leading Questions

When you watch a courtroom drama, it never fails that at some point during a witness questioning scene, the judge will hammer his gavel on the desk and object that one of the lawyers is "leading the witness."

Leading the witness can be terrible for a lawyer in a court, and even the best lawyers, knowing they will be stopped, will still do it from time-to-time, because they want the witness to think down a certain path.

In sales, asking leading questions can work hugely to our benefit.

We want our prospects to be thinking that working with us will be glorious, and working with the competitor, or even staying status quo, is one of the most terrible things they might imagine.

So what are leading questions?

Leading questions are questions asked to direct a specific response. They may be open-ended or closed-ended, but the goal is to get the client to agree with you on a specific purpose.

Unlike many simple open-ended questions which convey a lot in a few words, leading questions will typically have more substance to them.

A standard open-ended question would be, "How will this solution impact your business?" whereas a leading question asks, "How will this solution make your company **more profitable** and **efficient?**"

We want to force the prospect to think of the ways we are making them *more profitable and efficient.* Once we've dropped those specific words into the question, the prospect is now challenged to come up with answers which align with those words.

There is nothing wrong with asking the question as a standard open-ended question if you want a completely open conversation. But be aware. Finding out how the solution will impact the business may bring responses such as more work, another new process, training, slowing down areas for a while or whatever ideas the client may project on any new solution.

Early in the sales cycle, we want to encourage our prospects to make their own judgements and form their own opinions. This allows us to understand where they are leaning.

It allows us as sellers to hear their truths and listen to see if we are connected with their values. If we use leading questions before the client is lead qualified, we may not fully understand the client's ambitions and goals without our intervention.

However, as the sales cycle moves forward and new opinions and other vendors become involved in the process, what may have been a natural answer from a buyer may start to become hazy. With multiple different opinions from influencers, decisionmakers, competitors and anyone else who has something to say about the new offering, the buyer may start having a hard time articulating and understanding what they are actually feeling about you and your product or service.

Leading questions can help to steer the conversation in the right direction.

When we ask a leading question, we are placing a pre-formed opinion inside the question to steer a specific answer.

For instance, one of my recent students, Shona, is a high-end personal trainer. She is considered the celebrity personal trainer for those not (currently) living the celebrity life. Her services are very personalized and specific, and as such, so is the investment. Early on in the sales conversations her potential clients ask what makes her different from the results they would receive from doing a group fitness program or attending a low-cost gym with the promise of personal training assistance. These types of questions make her cringe, and rightly so. It's like looking at a bottle of champagne and asking what is the difference between the champagne and a low-priced six-pack of beer. It does the same job, right?

"How do I let them know what I do is completely different?" Shona asked me.

Like any sales process, it's not about what we tell our clients, it's about what we *ask* them and they tell us. When we start telling our clients what we do and why we are different, it may fall on deaf ears. The client hears what they want to hear and then they move on. Most of the time, what they want to hear is that they are going to get a better-quality product for the same amount or even less. Who wouldn't jump at that? But that's not real. Even if that was the case, the seller would find themselves in one of two different situations: either they are so overwhelmed with clients who aren't paying nearly enough, or the clients they do have don't respect getting a high-quality product which requires a premium process and service.

My response to Shona was, "What is the biggest difference between working out with you versus a group fitness class?"

"Well," she said, "I customize a program specifically for them. I allow them to listen to the music that most motivates them. I help them with their nutrition to maximize their fitness results. And really, I help keep them accountable."

I then asked her, "What question could you *ask* to help the person steer their own conclusion and see that you are different?"

Together we formed the perfect leading question which would both get her differentiator across while having the answer come from the prospect.

She came up with some great suggestions:

What experience do you have working with other personal trainers?

What results will you achieve by working with a dedicated personal trainer that you wouldn't get in a group fitness class?

How will working with a personal trainer help you achieve your goals faster?

Now we were getting somewhere!

By forming the questions in a way that forces the prospect to think about how their results will be better by working with her, she allows the prospect to plant the seed that the results they will get with her will be better and faster than anything they could get anywhere else.

Leading questions are great when used strategically to push an opinion on a client without overtly saying so. When the client has to create their own answers, it holds more truth for that individual and allows you to understand what is most important to them through the words they use in responding.

Know Where You Are

Karen had heard me speak before and we'd had a couple of calls around sales strategy and how to help close her deals faster. After two calls, Karen decided she didn't need sales training because now she was involved in a sales cycle which was likely to close "any day now."

Unfortunately for Karen, *any day now* dragged on for months. After being in a sales cycle with one client who was "close to close" for almost three months, she decided to give me a call and ask for guidance on her sales cycle. She wanted to know some negotiation tactics I would use to finally close her client. She sold a software and had given the client three demos on how the software might be implemented. She sent screenshots, and yet for four months, her prospect had still not moved forward to commit to the deal.

She'd asked all sorts of questions around how to close them, what could she add to the deal and how to properly negotiate the final contract signing.

However, before I would answer her questions, I wanted to know more about the meetings and demos she'd had. Although she was focused on the close, I wanted to learn more about the entire sales cycle, because when the information was presented, she may not actually be at deal-closed stage. She might still be earlier in her sales cycle and not know it.

What I found out was she was doing everything the client was asking of her and was not focused on taking care of her own agenda. The client would ask for information and she'd immediately send it without asking what they were specifically looking for. The client requested a demo and she would book one without asking what they would need to see in the demo for it to make sense. And when that last demo didn't show them exactly what they thought they needed to see, they booked another and another and another.

Without a plan or focus on the information she needed to receive from the client for the software solution to make sense to the client, she'd allowed herself to become a victim of her own sales cycle, or lack of. She'd allowed her client to lead the conversation and tell her what they needed to see next. But without knowing what their clear challenges were, what their goals were in having a better system in place, they requested information hoping the next piece of information, or demo, or screenshot, would be the light for which they were searching. And Karen was happy to provide them what they thought they needed without knowing herself what they were actually seeking. It was a classic case of the blind leading the blind.

Karen never challenged the conversation. Nor did she ever ask any of the right questions.

When I asked her if she'd covered any of the Lead Qualification questions, or BANT (more on this in the chapter Lead Qualification), she snapped back that the client was fully-qualified. She said she was dealing with the decisionmaker and they had budget (after all, her solution was only a small investment). She was pretty sure she understood why they were looking at the software and they'd said they wanted to make a decision by September. It was already September 2nd when we connected.

"But why?" I asked her.

"Why, what?" she'd responded.

"Why September? What is happening then that they need to make a decision?"

"That's just what they said.".

We were in deadly territory. We had a flaky decision deadline without knowing the reasons why the client had chosen that timeframe and when they wanted to make the decision.

There was no sense of urgency for the client to move forward.

Without a sense of urgency, the client sits back and it becomes a conversation around *hurry up and wait*.

In Karen's case, the client had decided they needed their information when they needed it. Karen would respond back quickly hoping this was the last thing they needed in order to move the deal to the contract phase. But it never was.

If Karen took a step back, she would be able to ask herself critically if she really did have all the information she needed.

When you get lost and don't know where you are in the sales process, default back to asking yourself, *Do I know everything about the client to make this make sense?* What else can you find out about the client's motivations and goals to help this process along? If the answers aren't clear, then invite the client into the conversation. After all, no one knows the client better than they know themselves.

What else do you need to see?
What are you unclear on?
How can I help you make this decision?
What other questions do you have?
What's holding you back?

It's better to have asked the question than never to have asked at all. You could spend agonizing days or months trying to read the mind of your client. Or you could go right to the source and find out for certain.

Chapter Thirteen

Transportation versus Destination

W hen you see an airline commercial, there's usually only two main scenes in the commercial--where you are and where you want to be.

The airline company will usually start out by showing you how terrible it is where you currently are. This isn't just Chicago any time of the year. This is Chicago in the middle of February. The bitter cold winter. All the snow and ice. And some frustrated woman has to warm up her car and now her car won't start. She brushes several inches of snow off the roof of her car and struggles to scrape the thick layer of ice off her windshield. Then, when she does enter her car, she's stuck in traffic during the middle of a snowstorm. This woman caps off her day, like she does every day, sitting at her desk crying about the long dark days and the bleakness of winter. She wants to be *anywhere* but here.

In a flash, the next scene becomes the beaches of Cancun. There's a hammock swaying in the light ocean breeze and the sound of the waves rolling on the white, sandy beaches. She is walking in an airy sundress, barefoot, the sun beaming on her. She is holding onto a tropical drink, smiling and laughing. *Ahhh...this is paradise.*

What does the airline *actually* sell?

I'll ask this question when I am presenting to teams or I'm on stage. And without fail, the first answers coming from the audience will be *dreams* or *experiences.*

But no one walks up to the ticket counter at an airport and says, "I would like one dream, please."

Airlines sell seats on a plane.

At no time in the commercial do they mention how lovely their gray leather seats are on their planes. They don't mention how smooth the seatback trays lower down. They don't talk about how they will fly 30,000 feet in the air for approximately four-and-a-half hours and how they usually get to their destinations on time, but if they don't, you can always take the edge off the air travel by purchasing one of their many (very) overpriced drinks from the flight attendant.

When airlines sell you a flight, they don't focus on the transportation or the process you will take to get to your location. Instead, they focus entirely on the destination. Where you are going and *who* you will be once you are there. The second part, the *who*, is very critical, no matter if you are referring to business-to-business or business-to-consumer.

As sellers, when speaking to our prospect, we typically talk entirely about the transportation. We focus on what it will look like as we are going through the process. We talk about our experience. We talk about how long it will take to get there. We talk about why they should work with us.

But our clients don't care about any of that. The only time the transportation, or the *how you are going to get me where I need to go*, conversation matters is only AFTER the client has agreed on where they will ultimately be once they work with us.

If you spend your time speaking with the client about the entire process before you and your client have agreed on where you will ultimately go, you risk talking yourself out of the deal.

The client wants to work with the provider who makes it easy. They have spent too much time coming to the conclusion that they have an issue which needs a resolution. They likely spent hours trying to figure out what they need to do to fix it and how it will be done. Now they have decided they need to go to outside sources for help. They don't want to know everything another party will do to solve their problem, they just want to know it will be resolved, and working with you will help make their business (or life) better off in the long run.

They already recognize how hard it will be. And if they knew exactly what they needed to do, they would have done it already.

They are coming to you because they want someone to get them there sooner. Where they want to get to is their goal. They want to be at the sunny beach destination as quickly as possible and they want to know that the provider they decide to work with to get them there is focused on the same end destination as they are.

When clients ask a business what their product or service will do for them, most salespeople get caught in the trap of explaining the entire process and not where the product or service will ultimately get them.

Home builders will talk about the home building process.

Engineering firms will talk about the meetings they will have to outline scope of work, performance objectives and review points as they get closer to completion date.

Business consultants will talk about how many meetings they will have with the team about culture and transformation and the surveys and other metrics they will use to determine if that culture has begun to take hold.

When we focus on what we will do and how we will do it, the prospect becomes lost in the conversation. You may think by providing more detail and clarity, you are setting yourself apart as the expert and helping the prospect to understand why you, or your company, is the perfect partner to resolve their challenge. But to the prospect, the entire process sounds complicated. It sounds like a lot of work. It sounds like there is still a lot to it.

The process is confusing. And the confused mind says *no*.

I was looking to hire a marketing company to help me deliver online ads. I wanted to create more excitement about the presentations I hosted in various cities. When I go to a location, I want plenty of new people in the audience ready to learn about creating a high-value sales process to help them *Sell More. Faster.* I also wanted to create more excitement for those who have seen me or followed my content for a while.

I was sitting down with one gentleman who was describing his marketing process, how he created marketing personas and how he came to his methodology. He explained how he determines the right messaging and images and colors and videos to make the most of my investment. Then he started to explain to me how search engine optimization (SEO) worked and how he'd developed a process that works for him and his clients and how he would apply it to the projects we'd work on. And…you get my point.

This gentleman went on for almost the entire hour's meeting talking about how the process with him worked, but he never really answered my first question. "Do you think you'll be able to get me the audience numbers I need?"

He was so lost in explaining the process he forgot we were trying to get to a specific finish line.

As a consumer, I thought to myself, *If it's this hard to understand if he will be able to deliver the finished product, what will it be like to get answers from him if we were to work together?*

Outlining the process, the features of a product or the steps involved in delivering your service is like staring a complicated connect-the-dots. You can see the numbers and will find the next dot and the one after that, but you may not be able to make out what the image is until you're more than halfway through it. Whereas if you told someone what the dots will eventually lead to, it's a lot easier to see the entire image before drawing each line individually.

The prospect has a problem and they want their problem solved as quickly as possible. They are looking for the easiest solution--a solution which will solve all their problems and leave them in a better position. Whether that is with more customers, more money or more time.

What we need to do to help them on this destination conversation is to first understand where they currently are and how much it sucks for them to stay there, and then discover where they want to go.

What Your Client is Searching For

Our clients are more engaged than ever. Unless you have brought a potential issue to their attention, they have likely discovered they have a problem on their own. And often, it's not that they believe they have a problem, but that their current situation could be much better.

The client is searching for a better, faster, more efficient way of doing things. They are looking to decrease their costs. They are looking to increase their revenues and profits. They want more customers, or better customers, or fewer customers who are willing to pay them more for the work they already do.

And our clients have a pain. If our clients engage with us first, they have determined there is an irritation with their company or their process and they want to find something better.

The annoyance the client has is like a symptom in which they have gone online and tried to discover by what it could be caused. Our clients begin their search with a WebMD approach. They type in their symptoms and try to self-diagnose themselves.

How Pharmaceutical Commercials Engage

If you remember the commercials from back in the 90's and early 2000's, pharmaceutical ads used to be all over television. They would scroll through a wide variety of symptoms and get the viewer to connect with a few of them.

Do you have problems with:
Itchy skin?
Redness?

Dry eyes?

Irritability?

Trouble sleeping?

Annoying children?

Enjoying coffee?

And the list went on.

And then, if you said yes to any one of those, you may have Coffee-children-sleep-itis, which could potentially be cured with this drug, so see your doctor immediately and ask for a prescription.

Our clients are no different. They don't always know the root cause of their symptoms, they just know that what they are suffering from needs to be fixed. Symptoms which can be annoying build over time into something greater and cause bigger issues. Symptoms which, if they aren't treated, will cause their company stress and will prevent them from achieving their goals.

For instance, a company is looking for better candidates to fill the constantly open positions. They have experienced plenty of employee churn in the last several months and believe they just haven't found the right person for the job.

The symptom they want to solve is to find the right candidate. But the root cause may be anything from management issues, lack of clarity in what is involved in the role or what they test for during the interviewing process.

An HR company could have plenty of things about which to speak to the client, but if they're only interested in helping the client relieve the symptom of *finding the right talent* they will limit themselves to that conversation.

Will the client ever really be happy? Maybe. But more than likely, if there is a greater root cause issue which should be addressed, the company will be happy with the HR company temporarily--until the next one or two candidates don't work out. Now they have someone else to blame for their lack of employee retention.

That's why as sellers, when the prospect comes to us with the issue, we don't want to just immediately address their needs, nor do we want to jump into what could be potential root causes. That's a great way to end the conversation right away. After all, who wants to be told they're wrong? Rather, we first want to get the prospect to agree that we understand their problem.

When you go into a doctor with your list of symptoms you have printed out from WebMD, does the doctor take a look at the list and agree with your self-diagnosis? If that was the case, we would need far less qualified doctors than we have. The doctor wouldn't have to ask you any questions. They would look at your print-out from the Internet and your self-diagnosis and immediately start treating you according to what a website said.

As much as people love to know right away how to solve their problems, I don't know if anyone would feel confident with the doctor who didn't ask any follow-up questions and came to their own conclusion.

A good doctor, on the other hand, starts by asking you questions about your symptoms. When did you first notice this was a problem? What have you done in the past to treat it? How long did that work for you, if at all? What else have you noticed?

Only after the doctor has satisfied their full list of questions will they go ahead and provide what they believe to be the root cause. You have to believe the doctor now truly understands what your issues are before you will feel comfortable with any new diagnosis they provide you, which is almost always the case.

My Self-Diagnosis

In 2013, I wanted to run my first marathon. I was pumped and decided to join a running club to help me train. The race was to be in the third week of May, and in January, I started my training.

I trained through brutal conditions. Fierce cold, wind, snowy paths. There were days I wore layers of clothes to prevent myself from being attacked from the cold outside, only to come inside, strip down, and immediately climb into an ice bath to prevent my muscles from seizing. It was an uncomfortable process.

As race day came closer, training continued to challenge me. We would do hill training for weeks, and then transition to speed training.

It was during one of these weeks of speed training that things turned for the worse. I completed a sprint and felt something was off. I'd injured my knee.

It didn't affect me right away, but as the days progressed, my knee pain wasn't going away.

I'd read online how to alleviate knee pain. There were cold packs, hot packs, acetaminophen, rest, massage therapy, tape and everything in between. But still, my knee pain persisted.

As days turned to weeks, I was determined to get my knee pain better and finally decided to see a physical therapist.

He asked me lots of questions. When did the pain hurt the most? Where else did I feel pain? How often would it last?

Finally he told me the pain had nothing to do with my knee, but rather, my hip. My IT band, a tendon that runs from your hip to your knee, was weak, and my body was compensating for the weak hip by putting extra pressure on my knee. If I strengthened my hip, my knee would feel better.

This was a massive relief to me! I'd been searching for a solution to a problem which didn't really exist. It was only after I met with the expert, whom I knew truly understood all the pain I was suffering, did I get the solution for which I was looking.

If the physical therapist would have immediately told me to start strengthening my hip muscles without making me feel like my problem was fully understood, I would have never taken her advice. I would have thought she was crazy and continued to look for a new solution. Only because we went through all the symptoms I was suffering did I feel she knew how much pain my knee was causing me, and only then was I willing to listen to a new possible solution to the problem.

Our clients may be looking for a solution we provide, but before we jump into the way to solve their problem, take time to first understand from what they are suffering and feeling in this moment. Then we can discuss where we can help take them and where they will be when they arrive at their destination.

Take time to understand that their current state is terrible. Allow the client the space to explore what they have tried in the past, what they are feeling when they are here and how things will continue to dissolve unless they make a change. Only after that process is complete can we move the client conversation onto the next part--where they want to be.

Where Your Client wants to Be

Going back to the analogy of the airline, instead of focusing on air travel, as sellers, we need to focus on the destination. Where does the client want to be when we have finished the project we will be doing with/for them? If you are creating an ongoing project or relationship, help them to focus

on what it will be like to achieve the first major milestone--
implementation completed, a major achievement, the first
time they produce revenue, or whatever the first part of their
goal consists.

As we dig deeper with our clients we want to take their
vision of what it will be like to be finished working with us
past the superficial of what it will do, to what it will *feel* like,
and then ultimately how the client will become different and
better when that change is made.

The reason the airline commercials are so effective at
getting people ready to book their next holiday destination
isn't because they present Cancun as a destination (or what
you will do when you are there), but rather, they give you an
idea what it will *feel like* to be there, and if the commercial is
really good, how much better a person you will be after a
vacation.

When you're designing the end-destination for your client
with what it would be like to work with you, try to paint the
picture so it doesn't just cover what it will do for them, but
also what it will *feel like* and what they are now able to
become when they achieve that level of success.

For example, a personal trainer will change the image they
paint for a client by moving along this progression: how much
easier it will be to perform many different exercises to how
much better the client will *feel*, to the type of person the client
can now *become* with that increased feeling and ability to
achieve more. For instance, someone who was stronger and

felt better every morning could now become a more energetic parent, a future marathoner or maybe someone who is now confident enough to ask their boss for that raise.

In a business setting, imagine an IT firm painting the picture for a future client. They could tell the client that their customer could surf the website securely knowing they will be safe from viruses and different types of malware. They can help the potential client by saying the client will feel much safer knowing their important information is protected. Finally, when the IT firm becomes fully integrated into the client's system, the client can pride themselves on their level of security for their own customers' information, allowing them to be one of the top providers from which to choose when other companies are looking for security.

Whenever we think about making a change in our lives, we think about what it would *feel like* and the person we will become once that change has occurred. The process and the act of doing isn't nearly as appealing as the idea of the new person (or business) one will become.

The process of moving this conversation is to go from *Do, Feel, Be*. It won't be appropriate to bring every client conversation to who the person or business will *become* when the change is made, but I encourage you to try it with as many as you can. It's powerful. When you become something greater than you are now then the sale happens far easier.

Chapter Fourteen

The Power of Empathy

In my first job with Xerox, and subsequently every sales position I held after, the company always invested in a couple of days of training. This was always a grueling week. The managers typically said they'd invested heavily in this training and it was in our best interest to immerse ourselves completely in the training. This meant no phones, no emails and to be fully-engaged. And I do believe in immersive training, except they would ask us to devote the time we would be selling instead to training, and when I ended my day, I now had to do a ton of work to catch up.

But besides teaching in an ineffective format, these same instructors would teach us all about creating the most *effective* and "*bulletproof*" business case proposal. We would use logical reasoning and spent time determining how to focus the conversation on a valuable return on investment (ROI) for the client. We would list the reasons a company might choose to do business with us, rather than one of our competitors. Typically, this included us as sales reps pushing our leaders to provide even more competitive analysis, because somehow we believed part of the sale was about ensuring the client knew why they *shouldn't* choose anyone else. It was the original ABC--Anyone But the Competitor.

Yet despite creating these amazing business cases which logically made complete sense because the client was saving money or the numbers would provide growth for their company, the client would still say *no*.

WHY? What's there to say no to?

This was so frustrating for people like me. I'm driven by analytical data and understanding the opportunity cost of not moving forward. The numbers made sense. The client would be spending only slightly more, or sometimes even less than what they were currently spending, and yet that wasn't enough? What more did they want?

I challenged the client's ability to reason rationally. The client often needed to *think about it*--whatever that meant. And sometimes after sitting on the logic for a few weeks or a month, the client would eventually, and reluctantly, say *yes*. Other times, the deal just wouldn't come.

And it wasn't because they went with a competitor. Sometimes they chose to do nothing--despite all the logic.

As I became better in sales and moved into larger sales cycles which required more touch points, more relationship nurturing and more calmness in the process, I started to naturally become more of my authentic self. I was relationship-oriented. I spoke with my client's about their personal lives, about what was driving them, what they wanted their legacy to be with their company and their roles. Suddenly, my sales skyrocketed and I was selling more while enjoying the process more.

It was only after I started my own sales training company and did more research on the power of empathy did I realized what I was doing in my own sales cycles which I didn't articulate. I was being more empathetic.

Empathy was something that was never taught to me in any of the sales training I ever took as a salesperson. We focused so much on the other aspects of the sales cycles, such as prospecting, asking questions and writing amazing proposals, but empathy was never spoken about.

As the only female in the bullpen at Xerox out of 13 reps, I was often told to "check my emotions" and that what we were doing was "business, not personal." I fought my natural tendencies to connect more deeply with my clients and kept relationships at an arm's length away--being stoic and determined in the conversations I did have. I did well. But knowing what I know now, I wonder if I had the ability in those early years to move from good to great.

Becoming more empathetic has massive benefits. It sees our client as who they are--*people*. Yes, businesses are logical and rational, but behind every business is an illogical and irrational person. We make most decisions based on instinct. Harvard Business Review did this as a study and found that

95% of people will make their decisions subconsciously. Only when we ask people to insert logic into their decision-making process do we completely change the answer.

Malcolm Gladwell wrote all about this in his book *Blink*. People know what they want before they justify it to themselves.

And in sales, we say people buy with emotion and justify with logic.

People know what they want. If we force them to make a decision logically, we risk losing the deal altogether.

Empathy before Rapport

We've all seen the movie where the hostage negotiator talks the hostage-taker down. The first time he gets on the phone, he introduces himself and starts asking the bad guy about his dreams and what he is hoping to accomplish. The negotiator tries to connect with the bad guy's emotional state first, before he starts asking further questions about the bad guy's friends and family. The hostage negotiator does their best to try to keep the hostage taker in an even emotional state because they know bad decisions may be made if people are emotionally charged.

Now, I'm not saying that sales is exactly the same as hostage negotiations--although for some readers it may feel that way. What hostage negotiators do best is tap into the emotional state of the person with whom they are working first *before* small talk.

If you're feel angry, frustrated or fearful, you bring that emotional-state lens into the memories and ideas you currently have. You may not want to move forward on new ideas or may imagine people don't have your best interests in mind when bringing new ideas. Sometimes this is where we feel others are *just trying to sell us*.

On the other hand, if you are feeling excited, motivated and generally just good, you bring that lens to your decision-making, as well. Ideas may sound better than they are. You're more willing to take a risk. And you believe everything will *just work out*.

Sales training was often focused on building rapport before diving into a conversation. It was believed that by building a conversation structured around small talk, you could create enough camaraderie that the prospect would feel more open and honest about what was going on in their head.

Seller: *I can see from the photo on your desk that you like boats.*

Prospect: *Yes, I dream of owning one someday.*

Seller: *That's great. I like boats, too. Would you like to buy something?*

This is an over-simplified example, but the idea holds true. How would creating commonality make the prospect be more willing to buy?

There is truth that people continue to engage with those who they believe to be a lot like them. As human beings, we subconsciously associate with those who have the same thought processes and beliefs as we do. There are ways to mimic this in order to get people to continue to engage. But it's incorrect to believe creating rapport first is enough to get someone to immediately become engaged during the sales process. Rapport comes after the person has shown interest in order to keep the conversation flowing.

So what is the right way to start a conversation? With *empathy*.

Empathy is the connection we have with an individual when we feel our pain and suffering has been felt by the other person, as well. When we stub our toe and the person we are talking to tells us they know exactly how we feel because it's happened to them and it hurts, we feel connected. When we tell the other person we stubbed our toe and the other person provides a sympathetic response, "That sucks," and, "It should be good soon," we don't feel as connected to the person.

Some people confuse sympathy and empathy. Sympathy is feeling an arm's length away from the person. When we are sympathetic, we acknowledge that the person is in pain. When know they are in a jam. But typically, we don't do more than that. A pat on the back and a, "There, there."

Empathy, on the other hand, is when we connect with something deep inside ourselves and do our best to know what the other person is feeling, whether it's because we've felt that way at some point in our lives or because we can connect with an unrelated time which helps us imagine what the person is feeling.

When we work with our clients, we want to take time to understand what they may be feeling at various stages of their buyer's journey. Do this before you start to talk and the conversation will be that much more meaningful.

For instance, a client looking to get a new mortgage may be going through a range of emotions, even though they sound fine on the phone. If this is someone's first mortgage for their first house purchase, they may be nervous, scared, overwhelmed, excited, enthusiastic or may bounce between all those different emotions on a single call.

What emotional states do you believe your prospects go through when you are in a sales cycle with them?

Take time to understand what they may be going through before pushing forward to get them to logically buy your product. Logically, they may be convinced, but emotionally they're not sure. Now's the time to work with their emotions to help them move forward.

Businesses Buy on Logic, People Buy with Emotion

For years, researchers and marketers knew the power of emotion in regard to sales. However, many people in business-to-business sales believed using emotions in a business conversation was far from appropriate. Logic and reasoning should be enough.

Emotional sales conversations were often left to consumer sales. And those businesses did it right. They would play commercials which would leave the viewer in tears. Telecommunications companies made our hearts melt when we watched the grandparents seeing their grandchildren take their first steps over a video call. Airlines made us cry when we saw families hugging and crying at the airport. Insurance companies left us terrified to think the next phone call could be from our teenage children telling us they got into an accident--that they're okay, but the car isn't.

The old marketers used the saying, *If they're crying, they're buying.* And that was the goal. If you had the viewer in tears, they would likely immediately buy your product or service.

And those who sold into businesses would think, "That's great for the individuals, but it doesn't make sense for a business."

That's where we were wrong.

Yes, businesses are logical and rational. They take actions which make sense to their employees, their customers and their bottom line. But behind every logical business there is at least one illogical, irrational person. Businesses may be logical, but individuals are emotionally-driven creatures.

Instead of trying to fight this, it's time we embrace this-- because the lines between businesses as a box and businesses which are individually motivated and have personality are becoming blurred.

We need to do our part as sellers to ask ourselves: 1) What is the current emotional state of the person making this decision, and 2) In what ideal emotional state do we want that person to be?

In your next sales conversation, take time to list out what you think the person (or people) are feeling going into this conversation, with and without your solution in place. We also want to know how the client would ideally like to feel when the solution is in place. Language matters in these conversations, because someone who uses the word *good* may not mean the same as someone who uses the word *content*. Feel free to dive deeper into the conversation to capture even more value from the conversation and ideally help your client achieve what they are seeking. This goes beyond the best solution, but the best solution which makes the clients *feel* their absolute best.

When we work with the client, it's acceptable to change the questioning process to also include more of these emotionally-driven questions.

Questions such as:

How do you currently feel about where you are (or your company is)?

How will having a better solution make you feel?

How will you feel differently between where you are today and where you want to be in the future?

By incorporating more feeling questions into the value-creation process, we have the opportunity to start tapping into a solution which is greater than just the look of it. When people feel different about the solutions they've created, we now have the opportunity to become our best selves.

It's okay if asking *feeling* questions seems foreign to you, especially in business meetings. I invite you to try and keep trying. You will get better.

There are some individuals who, although you ask the question, it will be difficult for them to answer. My solution to this is instead of using the word *feel*, use the word *gut*. Such as, "What does your gut tell you?"

You won't get the same response as you would in a feeling question, but you will start to open up the conversation to the initial reaction of the prospect in order to help make their decision easier. Or at least to know which way they are leaning in the process. The idea is we want to know if we are likely going to win the deal or not. If the client's gut reaction says they like another proposal better or they are interested in another solution altogether, you as the seller have the option to continue to invest in this client or cut your losses and move on to the next prospect.

Who would You be if You Accomplished That?

As we move up in the powerful question pyramid, we move away from what our clients will be able to *do* with their new solution to how they will *feel* when they get there, to finally who the person or company will ultimately *become*.

Joseph Campbell described this in his book **The Power of Myth as The Hero's Journey.** For every great narrative, the protagonist hits a moment when something in their life needs to change. They are unhappy with their current situation. They have a desire to grow, and the conditions in which they are currently placed now feel like a confinement rather than a comfort. The hero decides to go out and challenge what is known, whether that is the dragons protecting the treasures that await, or (and not specifically stated in his book) the company which needs a more secure infrastructure. The hero goes on his or her conquest to struggle and eventually defeat the outside forces, to come back a braver, smarter, stronger person.

In our case, the hero is our client. They know there is a better world out there for them. It will be a struggle to meet with vendors, discover their weaknesses and ultimately face their biggest fears when it comes to change. As they go through this process, it will be messy, because all change is hard at the beginning. It will be messy in the middle and glorious at the end. Eventually, they will take the necessary steps to do what is right for them to become a better company, a better employer, a better employee, a better business owner, or whatever they desire.

To drive this conversation to what the client will become, we can ask the individuals or businesses we are working with:

What kind of legacy will that allow you to leave on your organization?

What kind of company will you want to become?

What will making that decision and seeing it through to the end allow you to accomplish for yourself and your next goal?

Who do you want to become when you achieve that?

What person will you be if you took that action?

It takes a moment for a question like that to process. The client may be thrown back with this type of questioning. After all, it's deep. And how many other IT firms want to know what will be the legacy of a company when they become more secure to their clients?

Your client will take some time to answer this. Respect the space. Allow the silence. Embrace it. Your best responses will come from this space.

And as the saying of Lao Tzu goes, "When I let go of what I am, I become what I might be."

Steven was a graduate of **KO Sales U**, and as much as he was enjoying the course and the process we taught, he wasn't seeing immediate and dramatic results with his clients. When we covered the module on the power of storytelling and empathy, things really clicked for him.

Steven specialized in civil engineering projects specific to indigenous communities. Most of his projects before starting the program had been small, need-based projects. For Steven, it was enough to keep the lights on and the doors open for his practice but not enough to really build into the engineering firm of which he dreamed.

As we covered the empathy section of the **KO Sales U** program and he was learning about the power of asking questions around feeling and becoming, he immediately incorporated those questions into his practice. He met with the leaders of the communities with which he was already working and start asking:

How would you feel to have a project which employed more of your community?

What kind of leader do you want to become for your people?

How would creating more high-value projects help you to achieve that?

Steven said his meetings immediately had a much deeper connection. They would last the same amount of time, but the conversation went in a direction that was far greater than he could ever imagine.

Steven ended up missing his last two classrooms for his cohort because he was too busy to continue. He said the questioning process changed so quickly for his business that a couple of the projects he was working on suddenly quadrupled in size and scope! Steven said he was grateful he had access to the content for a full year because that would give him more than enough time to catch up--that is, if he ever needed to.

Managing Your Own Emotions

When I first started in corporate sales, the lesson I was told to learn faster than any other was to *develop a tough skin*.

It was difficult to not take rejection personally. All through our lives, when we put ourselves out there, whether it's school, or dating, or going for the ideal job, when we're rejected, we take time to reflect and think, "How can *I* do that better?" We try to learn how to make ourselves into smarter, more attractive or better people, above all else.

Even the standard breakup line, "It's not you, it's me," just spews the idea that we didn't live up to the standards of our love interest.

Entering into corporate sales was no different. When a client refused to speak to me on the phone or refused another meeting, I thought it was something I'd said or didn't say. I would tell myself stories that I wasn't good enough and I needed to try harder. The irony was, if I tried "harder" I would do the client relationship damage because I was forcing something that just wasn't there.

So I had to learn to get strong. I was told to not take the rejection personally. When the client said *no*, they were saying *no* to the opportunity. They were saying *no* to the timing. They were saying *no* to where they were in their business. It was the true, "It's not you, it's me," line.

When I took the moment of rejection personally, it affected more than that sales cycle. It affected all the sales cycles around it. I'd tell myself the story that I was less than who I was. I was unable to help this individual or their company. I was wounded, and who could I help if I was less than everything I should be?

I would mope and dig deep, trying to move the next sales cycle forward. But all the rejection did was cause me to tell a story about who I was that wasn't true. When I entered into the next sales cycle feeling less than who I was, I wasn't bringing the very best of me.

So I had to learn to develop a *tough skin*. I realized if one rejection was causing me to be less than for every future client and sales conversation, I was doing ALL my clients a disservice. I was using one client's rejection to cause me to deliver a less-than-highest-value of service to all my clients.

One client tells me *no* and all the others get a less-than-full version of me.

When I was less than my full self, I wasn't selling anything to anyone. My energy was spent telling myself I was good. That I was helping people. That I was not a single rejection.

Emotions sit with us in a deeper way than thoughts.

I eventually learned to not take the rejection personally. Part of that was when I started to put the relationship of the client first, before the sale. The other part was when I started not to hold onto the rejection myself.

I found friends and colleagues I could trust. When I had one of those really bad calls or even a really bad day, I had a group of people I could lean into. Whether they worked with me or not (and actually I found more comfort with those with whom I didn't directly work), they were there for me. They had suffered the same as me and now they were doing better. We would talk about what I could try different or new, and that always brought up my spirits.

I still find comfort having a great group of people with whom I get to practice new techniques and can lean on when I am feeling frustrated.

Some people can manage on their own, and I completely respect that.

But no matter what, I recommend finding your own great group of people. Maybe that's at a meetup with business owners and professionals like you. Or maybe you decide you need more than just emotional sales support and you need help discovering a sales process that works for you with **KO Sales U**. That's why we built in the great community for our graduates. Life happens. And we want you to know that we're here for you and with you. Let's help each other to *Sell More. Faster.*

Chapter Fifteen

Presenting a Solution

There will come a time in the sales cycle when it's appropriate to start presenting a solution. Typically this doesn't come out of nowhere. Both you and the client are set up to be prepared to talk about a solution.

Up until this point, the client should be feeling this is a collaborative relationship. They should feel as if they are a part of the solution they are creating because ultimately, they are. No one wants to buy something they haven't themselves determined they need.

Being open to ideas and options is great early on in the sales cycle, but then there comes a time when you need to step into the driver's seat. Your client wants to hear from you on what the ultimate suggestion is.

When you do present the solution, switch your hat from being inclusive in creating the solution to becoming the expert in the space.

Usually the meeting (or just) before presenting the complete solution with the price, we will begin to discuss what the solution will ultimately look like.

This does not mean that we start talking about the transportation of the solution. We still talk about the destination and we now include a very high-level summary of what the solution will include.

Going back to the airline analogy, this is not talking about the speed, distance or the mechanics of how air travel works. Instead, it's saying you will take a plane which will take you 4 ½ hours to get to your destination. Unless the client asks for additional details, we don't have to go more into this. Keep it simple! If you're solution can't be repeated by a four-year-old you've probably put in too much detail.

Present a single solution. Present one option for the client to say *yes*. The more options you present, the more the client needs to consider, and then ultimately, the confused mind says *no*.

I was speaking with a woman who owned a float spa. Floatation spas are a unique experience for someone who is looking for a immersive experience. The individual gets into a personal pod filled with salt water, which is soundproof, lightproof and promises to give the user moments of complete peace as the salt water flotation makes one feel completely free.

She had plenty of drop-ins and wanted to move people towards a monthly membership program. She had two different options for the monthly service--once a week or twice a month. She also had three different monthly commitments--three months, six months and one year. Once someone had finished their first float, she would ask if they would be interested in coming back again. The person almost always said *yes*. Then she would pull out the card with the six different options listed out in a grid. *How many months would you like to join? How often do you want to come?* A price and discount were listed depending on the square in the grid. However, despite the person saying *yes* to wanting to come back again, they would then say they "needed to think about it" after being shown the pricing grid.

"Why is it the person says they want to come back again but then they say they will book when they are ready?" she asked me.

Simple. She gave too many options. The person was confused and overwhelmed and consequently decided on nothing.

Even with a single solution, this can become incredibly overwhelming for a client.

Robert owns a customized software and app-development company. He is an incredibly brilliant person and I imagine he looks at problems the same way Matt Damon solved them as his character in the movie Good Will Hunting. For most of us, we saw numbers and characters that made no sense. To

Robert, this source code could be manipulated to create the most amazing applications which thousands of people would download.

Before joining **KO Sales U,** Robert often met with his client to do an assessment on what kind of customized software or app they were looking for. He would spend a couple days trying to figure out the problem and then come back to the client with a solution.

He would present the client with an extensive plan of action which would include development and testing phases, potential problems that could affect the development time, and finally, the price, broken down in stages of development.

Robert knew he was the best developer for the job, and yet after all this work, he had less than a 50% chance of EVER getting the deal. And those deals he did get, the client often took the information and waited months and received additional competitive quotes. Oftentimes, by the time they made their decision, Robert's initial assessment needed several changes, which of course he would do free to charge to finally get the client to say *yes*.

Robert over-produced the solution he presented to his client. He was going to cover all the steps he outlined, but similar to an airline passenger not needing to know how a plane flies in order to buy the flight, Robert didn't need to explain source code to someone who just needed an app to place a food order with a restaurant.

Before we even present the potential solution, we need to ensure the client is fully prepared for the solution, they know what to expect and we are confident that anything presented meets their expectations.

Anchoring Expectations

Before we get to the point where we can formally present the client a solution, timeline and price, the client will typically ask us, "What do you think this will cost?" or, "How fast do you think you can deliver a solution?"

Out of nervousness, we will throw out an answer we think is the lowest price and the fastest timeline. I'll hear solution providers say things such as, "We start at…" or, "We can do it as fast as…"

When we tell a prospect a timeline or a price, the first number we throw out is usually the one that becomes sticky. It's the one that the client will always remember, and it could either work in our favor or against it.

Construction companies are terrible at this. If you want a kitchen renovation, you will have someone come in to give you a quote.

"I know this is just the estimate, but how long do you think this will take and what is the approximate cost?"

The person with the clipboard will then pull out their phone, do some quick math and respond, "We could have it done as fast as six weeks for about $20,000."

"That's great," you think to yourself.

But as one delay leads to another and another unexpected cost sneaks up, what you first thought of as being so *great* turns into a nightmare. How can someone who considers themselves to be a professional not prepare for all these unexpected turns? Especially knowing that these types of unexpected events happen more frequently than the estimator first led you to believe.

By the time the kitchen renovation is finished, it's taken 10 weeks and cost $30,000--much more than the expectations they'd set for you.

Talk about turning what should be a wonderful experience into one where you doubt your sanity to take on such a project - and if you love your new kitchen enough to ever recommend the construction company, or the process, to anyone else.

In this case, the company did a terrible job of setting expectations. How much different would your experience have been if the company instead said, "Most of our projects will take 10 weeks and $30,000, and in an ideal world, we may be able to do it as fast as six weeks and $20,000, but we won't know that until we start doing our demolition."

Any company can anchor better expectations for their clients. Years ago, I was flying back home with a layover in Minneapolis. As I approached my gate, I saw the big red sign that every traveler fears the most: *Flight Cancelled.*

It had already been a long couple of days working and this was the last thing I needed before going home. I walked over to the airline counter and asked the woman standing behind it what I could do about my flight? I just wanted to get home.

The woman tapped on her keyboard and said, "Well, Ms. Orlesky, we can guarantee you a flight on tomorrow's same-time flight," *tap, tap, tap,* on the keyboard, "or, if there's a possibility I can get you on the flight this afternoon, would that work better for you?"

"Of course," I exclaimed. "Please, do whatever you can."

I was happy. I knew what the expectations were, a guarantee in tomorrow's flight and a possibility of tonight's flight.

This might have been a completely different conversation if the woman would have said, "I may be able to get you on the flight this afternoon, and if that doesn't work, I can guarantee you on tomorrow's flight."

I would have been upset. Angry even. "I can't wait until tomorrow. Please. Do whatever you can to ensure you get me on this afternoon's flight."

When setting expectations for time commitments, it's always better to tell people the longest possible time frame and then deliver it faster.

When we promise a client something faster than we deliver, out of our control or not, each moment that passes leaves a sour taste for the client. They have high expectations for us when they decide to partner with us. They set up the next stage in their lives and businesses based on what we've told them we will have accomplished. And when we don't deliver on the timeframe we first establish, it turns a positive relationship into a sour one quickly.

Under promise and over deliver.

That same construction company that's doing the kitchen renovation may think by saying "As fast as six weeks and a realistic timeframe is 10 weeks," is the same as saying "10 weeks and as fast as 6 weeks," but this isn't the case. The client never hears the second part. They hear the first number first and that's it.

Set the client expectations for everything, from when you will get back to them to when you will have the contract completed for signature, to when will the project be delivered and implemented. We want to start with the longest time frame and then let them know in a best-case scenario we may also do it faster. The goal is to have happy clients, not ones who are going to jump at our speed of work and then be immediately upset that it's not completed in the right time frame.

We also anchor for pricing. We became accustomed to saying the lowest price first and going up from there. Car dealers do this all the time. They tell you the car starts at a certain price. And unless you are a savvy car buyer, you know almost no car driven off the lot comes at that price tag.

The dealer has you purchasing an upgrade package, power windows, Bluetooth, heated and cooled seats, leather instead of cloth interior. And as each little check box gets ticked, you find you are no longer in the same ballpark as the first price posted. In some cases, you are almost double the original price.

When we anchor a client on time frame or price, we want to ensure we are setting realistic expectations. Even trying to sound more impressive with a fast time frame or a low price can sometimes work against our favor. Have you ever seen a price and doubted the quality is that good with such a low price?

I was working with a custom home builder and their team. We were talking about setting the correct price anchor. By setting a reasonable expectation for either price or time frame, we want to ensure we are setting the price correctly and then bringing the "deal" to the client if they are less than the average price or it becomes only a slight jump if the price is a bit higher. What we want to avoid at all costs is the sticker shock clients feel when the "base" price was nowhere near what the final price ends up. In the case of the luxury home builder's buyers, by setting a low anchor price, the buyer had to eliminate many of the features they'd wanted in the home, or they would have to go back to their bank and ask for more financing. All of which will lead to delays to get the final paperwork signed.

Then the home builder told me a story about a time when talking about price became a losing deal for them.

A gentleman booked a home tour with one of their consultants. Together, the home builder and potential buyer walked from room to room, talking about the finishes and features, all the little details which are given special care when one buys a custom home. As the two finished the tour, the consultant saw the smile on the man's face getting bigger and brighter. The last room on the tour was the dining room, where the consultant invites the prospective buyer to sit down as they go through the entire package and they ask the buyer to commit to putting down a deposit to start their own home-building process.

The man sits down and the first thing he says is, "I just have one quick question. What are your homes worth?"

The home they'd walked through was their flagship $3.1M home. The consultant, not wanting to turn the man off from the process of committing to build his own dream home, said, "Our homes start at $1.2M and go up from there."

The man immediately got up. "I'm so sorry I wasted your time. I thought you built better houses than that." And he walked out of the room.

For the most part, until you are comfortable with your price offering, try to avoid answering the question if the client asks "What's your price?" Many solution providers can vary in price dramatically, which will vary the price. When you're unsure on the complete solution you may provide the client, it's better to answer the question with, "All of our solutions are customized to our individual clients, and until we explore further, it wouldn't be appropriate for me to give you an incorrect range in price."

If the client is insistent on getting an introductory price, start with the highest price, or even the average price people pay, and continue the conversation. Even as high-value providers, don't be scared if your price is higher than the average market or your competitors. When you are providing an exceptional level of service to a client, they will buy. One of my favorite quotes is, "People may not have the budget, but that won't stop them from buying."

If your pricing is static and doesn't involve a lot of customization, feel free to open up the conversation. But don't leave it there. Price is heavy and we need to lift up this anchor by explaining what else the client will be receiving for their investment.

As long as the conversation with the client continues, the client is still interested. Yes, it may be out of their price range at the initial conversation, but your only goal in this process is to get the next meeting, and the one right after that, not to have them jump at the price point. If they do, that's a big sign you are priced too low.

In the case of the custom home builder, what they should have said was, "This home is priced at $3.1M. We have been known to create homes as low as $1.2M, depending on size and features." The client becomes anchored on the higher price. If, after they are finished the design process and picking out their custom features and the price comes out to $2.8M, the client feels like they got a deal! This is great! However, if the client was anchored at $1.2M, they would feel like a $2.8M price tag is absurd. That's over double what they thought.

The salesperson ends up having to do almost a completely new sales cycle again. The first time to get the client to buy into the process of building the house to begin with and the second time to try to sell on the new established price.

Don't rush through the pricing conversation until you are comfortable and are able to set expectations correctly. Take time practicing how to approach different pricing conversations and client questions. Role playing becomes invaluable in this scenario. It may sound great in your head, but the moment you say it out loud, the words can be easily fumbled. Find a few friends to practice with. Our team is also here to support you through practicing this and all of the other techniques you have learned throughout this book. Reach out! Tell us your success. Let us know other things you've tried. We honestly LOVE hearing how this information has helped you *Sell More. Faster.*

Determining ROI

Price by itself is meaningless. Imagine you were selling a car. You could list the price at $10,000 or at $80,000. What's the difference?

That's a huge gap for a buyer to decide on.

Now, there are cars that are worth either $10,000 or $80,000 but then the price is justified by what condition the car is in, what the quality of the manufacturer is, the mileage the car gets, and so on.

It's easy for a buyer to justify $80,000 on a high-end luxury car. The quality is much higher, the service is better, the parts last longer, and so on.

But if I was trying to sell a high-end luxury car for $10,000, people would seriously consider what's wrong with it. On the flip side, I couldn't expect to sell a five-year-old domestic SUV for $80,000, even if it was owned by me. I like to delusion myself into believing my ownership adds value to the vehicle.

It's not about the price. It's what the client will receive for that price. That's why we never present price as the end.

People are also forgetful. And even if we went ahead and told the client everything they would receive for that value, the price will land, and it's as if we used an eraser on the whole conversation.

It's price and, and, and.

It's the price and the return on that investment.

Oftentimes business owners struggle with this. How do you tell a client what they will actually receive after they pay that price? I'll typically hear comments like:
"I don't want to make any promises."
"I can't guarantee anything."
"I don't know how to measure it."

The ROI (return on investment) isn't up to you as the solution provider to tell the client what it will be. It's up to you to continue to question the client until they tell you.

Determining the ROI comes from the questions we started to develop in the Needs portion of BANT.
What would having a solution like this mean to you?
How much more revenue will you create in your business?
How many more clients do you believe you will be able to bring in when you're able to do this process faster/cheaper/more efficiently?
What is the increase in profitability you believe will be contributed to your bottom line?
What would you do with that time savings?

The idea behind understanding the ROI for a client is to continue to question them until they provide a quantifiable dollar amount that will be attributed *after* the solution has been in place.

When we're ready to formally provide the client the price in the proposal, now we have all of the additional *ands* the client has told us they *believe* to be true. And it's perfectly okay to present someone else's beliefs to them.

For instance, when I'm working with a company to provide their entire team sales training, we talk about all the same things I've outlined in this book. We go over their current state and what it feels like to be there. We discuss where they want to be and how what they feel right now will change when they are in this new life. Finally, I will ask, "And what will that do for your business?"

This conversation will take a wide variety of turns. The client may talk about some of the qualitative results, such as having happier employees and being able to predict cash flow months in advance. They may talk about quantitative results, such as increasing their close ratio, improving their sale open-to-close time frame or increasing their average dollar-per-sale.

When the time comes for me to present price for the sales training, I will introduce the price and continue talking about all the additional features such as, "And this will provide you with greater cash flow predictability and your close ratio will improve. And as long as the leaders of the team continue to work with the individual reps, I fully expect your average dollar-per-sale to increase".

At no point did I make any promises. There's still a lot left up to the client. I know they will see improvements in those various areas because almost all my clients see an improvement there. But I didn't say how much or how quickly. That's out of my control. What is in my control is to teach a process and strategy. What they do with it is up to them. But if continued on correctly, it will provide them the results they are looking for every time.

Thinking vs. Assuming

The reason we ask clients so many questions is because we need to *know* what is going on with them. Who knows our clients the best? The clients!

When I'm working with one of my one-on-one clients and we are strategizing and planning the next steps for sales meetings, ensuring we have everything we need for the proposal stage of the sales cycles, I'll typically start peppering my client with lots of questions. We go through BANT and try to determine the return on investment (ROI) the client needs to see. We work on finding the best solution for the client. All through this, the moment a response comes back from my client that, "I think the company wants to see this…" I stop the conversation.

Thinking is deadly when it comes to a sales cycle. You are supposed to be your client's savior. You are the expert in your space. And when it comes time to present and place a recommendation, are you going to *think* you know the proper solution, or will you *know* you have the proper solution? How many experts do you know who just *think* they know what a solution will be for a problem?

If I was to go into surgery, and before I was put under, the doctor started using phrases like, "I think this is the problem you are having," and then, "I think the best solution will be for us to remove your appendix," I would lose it! I would immediately be jumping off that bed and looking for a new doctor.

I don't want someone who *thinks* they know what the problem is. I want to find someone who has asked all the right questions, has done their research, completed their assessments and tests and now *knows* with a certain level of confidence both what the problem is and what the best solution is. I want someone who has done this before, or if not exactly, has so much experience that their skills are easily transferable in providing this new solution. I want to feel comfortable that I am going to be well taken care of and I will be better off in the end.

I had two partners in an engineering firm come into my office one day. They explained to me that they had several meetings with a very large client and they needed to hire me to "close the deal." They proceeded to tell me they had already done "99% of the work" and the "last 1%--the close" was going to be up to me. I tried to stifle my laugh. First of all, the close is not the last 1%. It's the last 100%. If you don't have a closed deal, you have nothing. You've done all this work for no revenue. Secondly, the close isn't something that just "happens." There is no magic wording in which I walk into a boardroom, say two sentences, throw down a contract and leave. The close starts from the very first meeting.

If sales is like dating, it isn't about having someone else come in and propose to your spouse for you, it's about the journey you take together with your future husband or wife. It's about all the dates you go on together, all the memories you have with your loved one and the confidence you have in each other that you will get through the next years and decades and still love each other.

Despite this, I genuinely wanted to help these men. I knew they needed to understand the entire sales process and strategy to give them an awakening into what sales really is. So I turned to the words of Zig Ziglar. "You can have everything you want in the world when you help enough other people get what they want." (Which by the way, became our #1 corporate value at **KO Advantage Group**.) I knew I needed to help them.

I started asking them questions about why they thought they had already completed "99%" of the journey. With whom were they meeting? What was that person's role in the decision-making process? Who else would be involved?

As I asked the questions, I knew immediately they were a lot farther behind than they thought they were. The answers were coming back, "I think...", "I think...", "I think..." Oh, no. They didn't actually know where they were or their client was in the sales process. They were spending too much time thinking they knew the answers and not enough time actually confirming what they *thought* they knew. These gentlemen weren't at the closing stage of the sales journey. They were barely at the lead qualification stage. Just because the company is a large organization doesn't give them a pass to be automatically qualified as a sales cycle. You still have to do all the same work.

Oftentimes, people don't want to ask the questions they *think* they already know the answers to because they don't want to come across as looking dumb or ignorant. That's simply not true. I would much rather have someone ask me directly and know with certainty what is going on in my business, who else am I speaking with and how am I determining whether this was a worthwhile project than *thinking* they know the answers.

Thinking without knowing is the sign of an amateur. Experts want to know with certainty. Fools want to act by thinking they already know all the information.

In your sales cycles, go through all the lead qualification questions and ask yourself truthfully, "Do I *know* this to be true? Or do I *think* it is?"

When you *think* you know and answer, or can honestly say to yourself that you don't know the full answer from the client, start writing these questions down. If it's one or two questions, feel free to call or email the prospect and ask them. By this point, you should have developed a relationship with the potential client enough that it will become a fairly seamless conversation.

If you realize there are still a lot of questions which are still not known with 100% certainty, this is a great reason to book another meeting. You will have the opportunity to explore more with the client and ultimately you will be seen as a better service provider in their eyes because you took the time to truly care.

Don't feel embarrassed by asking more questions. If someone was trying to sell me a solution, hands down I would rather they know all the pertinent information rather than to try to present a proposal with far too many unknowns.

As for the two engineers? They didn't believe me when I said they were weren't ready for proposal stage because they didn't know enough about their client yet. They left and continued on meeting with their prospect. And meeting again, and again and again. It was over three months later when I heard from them again. Now, who they thought was the decisionmaker had changed to a new position, the scope of work they created for the client was sitting on someone's desk and they were waiting for some type of next step from the client without knowing what that next step was. They were no further ahead with the client, and because so many things had changed, they weren't even in the same sales cycle. But they didn't believe me when I said that, either. On the positive, they also weren't any further behind, because they weren't nearly as close as they *thought* they were. Maybe one day they'll get the deal, when they are willing to admit the client knows more about themselves than they know about what the client needs.

Chapter Sixteen

Proposals

The time has come for that glorious moment of the proposal! Congratulations!

I will often compare the proposal stage in a sales cycle as the proposal stage in a romantic relationship. It often doesn't just appear out of nowhere. It typically doesn't happen if both people don't know everything (or at least everything that's important in this relationship) about each other. It's a beautiful moment. And it's one that was well thought out and planned before it comes forward.

The proposal is as much a part of your sales cycle as any other area, and as such should be given special attention.

However I see too many people get to proposal stage and think they're done. Present it or send it and hope for the best.

People will put together a presentation, email it to the client, or if they do take an extra step, they'll visit the client and present the proposal without a thought on going forward.

If you were dating someone and decided to propose to them, would you move forward if you honestly thought there was a 50% chance or greater of them saying *no*? Would you do it over email?

Hopefully you said no, or at least laughed at the thought.

If you wouldn't do that with someone with whom you want to spend the rest of your life, why would you do that with a client with whom you hopefully want to create a long-term relationship?

It didn't matter if I was selling a $4,000 high-end desktop printer or a $40M global payments solution. The proposal was always the same.

I have people ask me what I recommend as the best proposal software. That's ridiculous! Why do you need a proposal software to fill in all that information?

Your proposal should be customized to your client, and there's no software that is going to do that for you. You have to devote focus and know what your client needs first before developing anything. If you don't know what your client's goals are or don't understand where they want to be, it doesn't matter whether you create the proposal yourself or use a software solution--you're never going to get the deal.

Since the proposal is a story, it needs to be presented as such. The proposal is not a scope of work, a letter of engagement or a contract. Those documents have their own words for exactly what they are. The proposal is a proposal. It is a story. It is a moment. And it needs to be delivered clearly and walked through with the client to ensure the value is shared between both of you.

Delivering the Proposal

When someone proposes to their significant other, it's usually presented in a way that summarizes the entire relationship up to this time. All the wonderful moments they've shared. All the loving dates they went on. The funniest moments. "And now I would like this story to continue as we grow old together." The person receiving all these loving words says yes because the couple's story is just beginning. They want more.

The proposal we deliver to a client is a story. It is a summary of the journey we have just been on with our client. This is a tender moment, and like a romantic proposal, it's the first day of the rest of our lives (or at least the life of the client-supplier relationship).

If I was being asked to marry someone, the proposal would be a great indication of how the marriage would ultimately be. Was it thought out? Was it meaningful? Did I want this moment, and future moments, to continue?

The proposal is an expected meeting. This is not something that is "sprung" on the client. It should be booked in the calendar with both you and the client, with the meeting subject line: Proposed Solution or Proposal Review, or some other defining meeting.

We book the meeting by preparing the client with the knowledge that our next meeting will be, "to present to you everything you need in order to make a <u>decision</u>." This is important.

At this point, we change the focus from being open to everything the client has to say to being focused on being the expert and presenting the client with the next step in the process.

We are still very much interested in the client, but the shift is now to have the client interested in what you've learned about them as opposed to what you are still learning about them. Subtle and significant.

The client is now open to how you will summarize their struggle and what you believe is the ideal solution. If they already knew what they needed to do in order to achieve their goals the quickest, they would have already done that. That's why you became such a huge part of their journey and discussion. Now they need you to tell them what they need to do. They can't do it alone.

The proposal should ideally always be delivered in person. Full stop.

You want to be able to converse about each part of the proposal, test for understanding and read the client's body language as you are going through the document.

If you can't deliver it physically in person due to geography or some other limiting factor, you should meet the client face-to-face with Zoom, Skype, Facetime or any other screen-sharing, video-conferencing software.

Share your screen as you walk through each page of the document. This way you have control of the conversation. A screen-share is not the same as emailing the proposal and talking through the document on the phone. You miss out too much of the body language that's so invaluable in a person-to-person meeting, and without visual, you don't know what your client's attention is on. Is it their phone? Email? Have they already skimmed through the proposal and now they're waiting for this call to be done?

If you are delivering the proposal in person, you can choose to present it on a screen for everyone in the room to enjoy. This is handy in the event there is more than one decisionmaker, or one decisionmaker and a few influencers as part of the conversation. However, I've always preferred to print off copies for everyone in the room. I will sit next to the main decisionmaker as we all walk through the document together. The entire process should have been a collaboration up to this point, so let's keep up the feeling that we are in this together. And together, we will walk through this document.

Be careful to not let anyone jump ahead of the story. It's like reading a book--skipping to the last few pages, finding out the main protagonist dies and then losing interest in the book. Since your proposal is your story, don't allow anyone to jump to the end. If someone does, turn it into a joke or let them know you'll take away the pages they don't need. People will generally smarten up and pay attention to you rather than the only piece they're interested in. You've taken a lot of time to get to know your client. It's easy to ask for the same respect in return.

Emailing the Proposal

This is an unbelievable no-no in my world. There is almost no reason a student can give me which makes it acceptable to email the proposal to the client without going through it together with them first.

When we email a proposal to a client, it's like saying, "I've had a great time getting to know you up until this point, and I wish I could care enough to walk through this incredibly important document with you, but I honestly don't care if you say yes or no."

The proposal is the most important moment in your sales cycle. You've spend hours, or weeks, or months, building up to this moment, and now you're going to reduce all that relationship-building time to an email?!

When my husband proposed to me, how likely do you think I would have jumped at the chance to say *yes* if it was sent via email? *Subject Line: Want to get Hitched?*

I would have been appalled! My girlfriends and I would have laughed about it for years to come.

And I probably would be back to single.

Our clients are no different.

If the relationship is valuable to you, then create valuable interactions. This is our final moment for us to showcase what it will be like once the client chooses to work with us.

The proposal is important to the relationship. Take care with it.

If the client asks you to "just email me the proposal," do everything you can to resist this. Emailing the proposal takes control away from you and puts it back on the client.

The moment they receive the proposal, where does the client go? To the last page. They look at the price and then determine whether it's worth reviewing again. You build so much into this relationship, and you're allowing this moment to be determined by the size of the engagement ring (in this case, the smaller the better).

If the client asks you for the proposal early on in the sales cycle, they typically aren't ready for the proposal. Most of the time they are unsure about the sales process and where they are in that process and decide to move to the proposal stage because once they find out the price they will better know where they are. Avoid this as much as you can. No one considered whether a university degree was worth pursuing based on the information in a single textbook. Especially for those of us offering high-value services, seeing a price point in the tens or hundreds of thousands won't help a client make a decision any faster. If anything, it will stall the decision-making process.

What I typically say if the client pushes for a proposal before I have all the information I need to fill out the proposal is, "I'd be happy to. When can we sit down and meet? I'd like to ensure the solution I'm putting together for you exactly meets your needs."

If the client refuses to meet with you for the proposal, ask yourself the serious question--if they're unwilling to sit down for the proposal, when will they be willing to sit down to put the solution together?

There was only one time in recent years where I felt I had no choice but to send the proposal to the client before we were ready for it.

I was working with a large enterprise account on bringing in sales training for one of their sales team divisions.

We had our initial meeting and discussed what sales training would look like, what they hoped to get out of it and what their team would be able to accomplish with the right training in place.

We left that meeting with the agreement of meeting again. Unfortunately, we couldn't lock down on a date before I left that first meeting because there were three other people involved in the decision-making process and two of them were out of town. We agreed on a couple tentative dates and would connect at the end of the week to formalize a time within those dates.

When I called back to get the time and meeting secured, the client *insisted* I send them a proposal for review. I pushed back, saying that I was still unclear on what they were looking for, and without the input of the decisionmakers, I would be completely unable to give them a solution that would exactly meet their desires. However, despite my insistence, there was no swaying this decision. Their minds were made up. And the other vendors were sending proposals anyway.

I said I would be happy to send *something,* but it was not to be taken as a full proposal, but rather a starting point.

As the seller, this becomes a tough place to be in.

Anything I put in front of the client now becomes sticky. There is little opportunity to increase the price, even when value is created. But because not enough value has been created at the beginning, price too high and you may be out before you even get started.

It's a tactic that many large companies will take because they know this game. And it's a dangerous one to play for both the buyer and the seller. When there isn't enough value created, when you are basing a majority of your decision on the right vendor based on price, you are unable to create a strong relationship you know will follow through the implementation of the service.

So I put something together.

I built my proposal the same way I would for any other client. I knew there were gaps in the conversation, and with that I built comments on the side of the proposal saying where additional clarification was needed. I struggled putting together the price. After all, I wasn't completely sure about the solution, and some of the things we were talking about in the initial meeting included areas on which I would still need to do additional work and research. When I sent it to the client, I made it very clear I would be calling to clarify the additional areas.

And I did.

I treated each phone call as if we were still in the sales cycle. Because we were.

Yes, they received the proposal, but that by no means meant we were at proposal phase. We were still in value creation.

They read the last few pages of the book and knew how it would end, did that mean that they weren't interested in reading the rest of the book? Absolutely not. We still needed to go through the journey and story.

I called and asked what their initial thoughts were and their gut reaction. I asked for clarification in the areas I was still unsure about, such as delivery dates and how we would measure our success together. I was always insistent on setting up a next meeting, even when days and travel schedules didn't always permit, but I always had to ask.

We continued to talk, but instead of each conversation being focused around "following up on the proposal," each 15 to 20-minute call would be focused around what more they would like to see. Why were some of the areas being presented by other vendors important to them? What did they ultimately want to achieve? And how would they know in the short-term and long-term they'd achieved that?

We weren't at proposal stage until I finally booked the in-person meeting. And of course, when they asked if I would like to do it in person or over the phone, I insisted it would be done in person. Because, only now, despite them seeing the proposal early, were we *actually* at proposal stage.

Sales is a relationship and both people need to agree where they are at in the relationship. Just because one person is dreaming of wedding dresses and engagement rings does not mean both people are ready for that stage. We may agree that's where we eventually want to arrive, but timing is everything on both sides of the relationship. And when we are walking together, side-by-side, then we can truly move things forward.

Don't be coerced by the client to rush to the proposal stage. If you do have to present a proposal early, call it what it actually is--a brochure with a price on it. It is not a proposal, because the proposal is the story, and until you are able to tell the story with the client, you are not there yet.

Go back into your sales cycle and ask yourself if you have covered your lead qualification questions. Have you created value with the client? If you haven't yet, then call it where you are in the sales cycle, not where you think you might be because you "submitted a proposal."

I had a gentleman sit in on one of my presentation and tell me he was calling on companies, and this very large company had asked him to send them a proposal and they would get back to him if they were interested. He asked me, "What do I do now?"

I told him to call it what it is. He'd sent a lengthy brochure with a price.

He insisted he'd sent them the full proposal.

"I understand what you *think* you sent them," I said. "But do you know who's going to be making the decision? Do you know why they need to change? Do you know when they are making a decision and what the impact will be to their company if they don't make a decision?"

"No," he replied.

"Then you're not at proposal stage. You threw some crap on the wall and hoped something would stick."

Call a spade a spade. You're not at proposal stage until *both* parties agree you're at proposal stage.

I told him his next steps would be to continue to insist on a meeting in order to go through the lead qualification process and move through the sales cycle appropriately.

No one is going to buy just because they are holding onto the brochure, even if it has the price. They still have questions and will ask, "How would this apply and impact my business?"

Putting Together the Proposal

My proposals have stayed the same for years, and now it's the same template we teach our student in **KO Sales U**: six slides covering the most important aspects of the solution.

Do not overcomplicate this process. The proposal is your story to the client. Tell it as such--the summary of the journey we have gone on together.

Every interaction, every question, up to this point leads to ensuring the proposal document has everything you need to help the client make the best decision for themselves and their business.

Before finalizing and presenting the proposal, think like your customer and ask yourself, *What's stopping me from saying yes?*

The whole purpose of the sales cycle is to put together the proposal in a way that communicates the entire vision and strategy of moving forward with the client.

The more time we spend with the client, the more information we will have to put into the proposal. Our questions inside the value-creation phase of the sales cycle are all directed toward ensuring you have a well-thought-out proposal.

Goals

The goals of the client are the first place we want to focus the conversation. This is simply the overarching goals, our product or service aside.

We want to cover the goals because this is an incredibly easy way to get the client to agree immediately.

We are telling the client simply--*We know where you want to go and we've outlined it here for you.*

Does the client want to grow their business 25% year-over-year? Do they want to be seen as the market leader in their industry? Are they targeting new geographies? Maybe they are wanting to achieve higher profit margins for their organization?

Whatever the client is looking for, this is the moment where it is outlined and agreed upon by the client.

Current State

This is a summary of where the client currently is and the ramifications of spending one more day where they currently are.

This will typically be covered somewhere in the value-creation stage with a question like, "What would it mean to your company if you don't change?"

This *has* to be information given by the client. If it is not, it doesn't matter how good the rest of your proposal is. The client isn't convinced their life will be worse off or needs to significantly change. The client will revert back to the status quo because things aren't as bad as they seem.

The current state should focus on all the reasons the client wants to change and what it could quantifiably mean to their business if they don't.

Ideal State

The focus then switches to where the client wants to be within the next six months to one year (or whatever the timeline is of your project). Try not to choose a timeline too far in the future. Even with construction timelines, which can take years to deliver, focus on the ultimate finish, but also one of the closer targets, such as awarding the contract, having all the designs in place and starting to break ground.

Anytime we bring a goal to a closer timeframe, such as six months or a year, it is much easier to picture its reality.

When someone thinks about where they will be this time next year, it is more appealing to start taking action now.

The Ideal State differs from the Goals, because the ideal state is after your product or service has been incorporated into the client's business. The Ideal State is usually a shorter timeframe than the goals, but it doesn't have to be. The Ideal State is also a small aspect of the client's business which will help them to achieve their goals in a larger scale.

Think of this like a restaurant. A restaurant wants to increase the number of people ordering from them in order to increase their revenue by 20% year-over-year. You are selling them a food delivery service. Since they are limited by the number of seats they have in the restaurant, they can't realistically increase their revenue by much with their current state. They are limited by seating. During peak times, they are already packed with a waiting list and they need to find a new source of revenue. Their Goals may be to franchise or open more locations. However, in their Ideal State, they could offer customers a new way of ordering food from the restaurant by providing food delivery, which will allow the restaurant the ability to serve more customers without having to increase their footprint earlier than when they are financially prepared.

The Ideal State covers the 30,000-foot view without going too into depth on what the solution will actually look like. We save that for the next slide. We want the client at this point to say, from a high-level, this solution could work for them.

Solution

Now that the client is getting an idea about what they can possibly achieve when everything is working perfectly in their new situation within the next few months to a year, we will start to describe the ideal solution.

The solution you present to the client should be clear, concise and with few options attached. We want to client to easily say *yes*. We don't need to go into too much detail with the solution, but rather present it in a bullet form.

The solution page will be more of a talking point. With each feature of the solution outlined, we need to speak about the reasons and benefits as to why someone would need that feature.

Do not list a feature if you are unsure of the benefit to the client.

The benefit could easily be broken down as, "because of this _____, you will be able to achieve this _____."

Going back to the restaurant example and selling a food delivery service, we could tell our clients, because we will be able to deliver meals to your customers within 30 minutes of ordering, you will be able to have high-quality food delivered right away while still having it arrive at the same level your clients would expect from your in-house dining experience.

If you do decide to provide options, ensure they are clearly outlined. Never present more than three options. If you do present more than one option, always present the most complete, comprehensive option first and then work your way down.

Similar to the way we anchored expectations for price and time frame, we want to anchor the best solution first. As we move from the Platinum to the Gold to the Silver solutions, the client has to ask themselves, *Can I do without this?* Instead of the opposite, *Do I really need to add that?*

It's much harder for someone to have things taken away from them than it is for them to decide to add.

By forcing a complete solution on just a single slide, you will focus only on the key points of the solution and not every detail. What isn't written can be spoken about. Focus on what absolutely NEEDS to be there. Not on every detail.

Timeline

As we learned in the lead qualification and correspondingly BANT, the Timeline is one of the most critical areas of the sales cycle.

It's not about when we start working with a client but rather when we end that is the focus of the proposal.

Understanding from the client when they want to see their project completed, when they want to have everything running perfectly and why that is important becomes the last day on our timeline. Then we work backward from there.

The last date, whether it is six weeks or six months from now, sets up the entire timeline.

The timeline should have no more than six points in it. Any more than that becomes too cumbersome to understand at a high level.

The timeline should also have no less than three points in it, because then it becomes too overly-simplified.

You will want to focus on the main points that will be measured while the implementation of your project is going forward, such as:

User trials, testing and adjustments

Completion Dates

Follow-up reviews

Start (and finish) of phase two, three and more of a project, if so warranted

Contract signing dates

Initial assessments

Each one of these points (and anything else critical to your unique business needs) is important to address as part of what you are creating with the client.

We want the client to understand that this is a comprehensive project and is more involved than they are able to do themselves, while not being so overwhelming that they feel they are getting in over their heads.

The timeline is a fine line we want to manage.

When we read the timeline to the client, we start with the farthest date out and bring ourselves backward to the closest date to today. With each point, we emphasize why it is important and its contribution to the project.

Return On Investment

When it's time for the proposal, the client only really cares about, "How much will this cost me?" That's why we build the story throughout the proposal to get to the investment. Don't rush to get to this page. The story, the consequences of not taking action, where the client ultimately wants to be, and how you're going to help them get there all contributes to the reasons why the client will be more willing to invest.

Most people will struggle with this phase of the proposal. They will try to rush through it, because talking about money is uncomfortable. If you're one of those people, then practice. Find some role-playing buddies. Send me or my team a message about how you can get more practice in various phases of your sales cycle through one of our programs. Or just sit by yourself and say it out loud again and again. Be great at delivering this information, because your client is expecting you to be the expert in creating them a solution, and part of that is knowing how much your expertise is worth.

Read again about Determining ROI with help on how to quantify this. As long as you've asked various questions on quantifying the result with your client, you should have all the information you need to deliver an outstanding price and its corresponding ROI.

Samples questions you may have asked at this point:

What will this solution do for your business?

How many more clients would you expect when this process is faster?

What is the increase in revenue will you capture when your employees are spending less time on this redundant task?

How much can you see your business growing after this is finished?

And so on.

The goal is to get the client to quantifiably tell us what they expect from the solution. This arms us with all the information we need in the ROI section of the proposal.

The more quantifiable information, the stronger the business case.

We can also use the qualitative solutions, such as being happier at work, being seen as a market leader, spending less time on repetitive tasks, and so on. However, when you do receive an answer from a client that doesn't have an immediate qualitative answer, do your best to continue to question until you get there.

Qualitative (the warm and fuzzy answers) are still good, they will just help to reinforce with a client that this is a great decision. Qualitative improvements should be presented after the quantitative ones.

When we do present the price, never land on it. Price is heavy. Present the price and then offer all the things the client will get *because* of their investment. We stack the price with "and."

For instance, when presenting price, we will say something along the lines of:

This entire solution will be brought to you for three payments   of $4,997, AND this will allow you to set your company up to be able to grow   your   business   20%   year-over-year, AND you will be able to gain that extra 50 clients per quarter as   your   goal, AND your employees will be happier because they get to focus what they love to do, with the rest being outsourced to my team.

"And" stacking the price takes the weight off the price and focuses the conversation on what they will get for that price.

Once the ROI is laid out in such a way, we take a small pause and then we test the waters to see how close the client is to making a decision. Usually a question like, "How does that sound?" works.

When asking that question, we are then asking *How does all this success sound?* The client should answer positively at this point. This will also become the typical point where the client will start bringing up objections. Welcome them! That means the client is critically thinking about your solution and ensuring it is the right fit for their business, which then will naturally lead you to the last slide: Next Steps.

Next Steps

Yes, I know I promised you a six-slide proposal, and with the addition of the Next Steps slide that now brings us to slide seven. I don't really count the Next Steps as a new slide because it is really the reiteration of the timeline, this time summarized into three points: Where we are today, when we sign the agreement, the length of time the project will last with outlined start and end dates (if they exist). Next Steps are focused on the agreement-to-completion. We want the client to know that since they have pretty much made a decision, now is the time to put pen to paper.

Don't be fearful of this moment. This is a good moment!

We've already prefaced the meeting as *providing you everything you need to make a decision*, and then we reiterated the reasons they need to change. We've provided them a solution, which they then agreed (even after an objection or two) sounds good. Now we ask them our closing question: *Are you ready to move forward on this today?*

If the solution is being presented to the ultimate signing authority and you know they can move forward, then place inside your Next Steps that the agreement will be signed today. If you know they will need to go back to their decisionmaker or a couple of influencers to get another opinion on whether this is the right solution, state the agreement needs to be signed within two weeks from now.

There should be NO circumstance where a proposal is presented and the decision needs to be delayed for a month or two, or more.

Too many things will change in a month and beyond, and you want to ensure the level of excitement and a sense of urgency is still present.

I've never had a proposal where the decision to move forward took longer than a couple of weeks. If that's the case, then you either are not ready to present the proposal, or what you are presenting isn't really a proposal. It's really a first round of information.

If before the proposal meeting, the client says to you they will still need to review it with others, then ask them to either include them in this proposal meeting or book their internal meeting immediately following yours.

If you're at proposal stage, there shouldn't be any more reason to wait on moving forward. The phrase to live by is, *Strike when the iron is hot.* You want to ensure motion is being carried out quickly and with purpose until the deal is actually closed.

Having the client give you a verbal commitment to move forward is a LOT different than having a contract signed and payment processed. A verbal agreement is not the same as a signed agreement. Do not celebrate verbals.

I've had deals never move through after the verbal because something changed on the client's end.

We celebrate when the contract is signed and payment has been arranged.

Closing Question

As the proposal is being wrapped up, all the information has been presented to the client and the timeline to move forward has been presented as today or in the near future, it's time to ask our final closing question.

The closing question is a very direct and poignant question asked to incite a "yes" answer. The closing questions is time specific and oriented towards taking immediate action. Try a few different versions of the closing question and find one that feels comfortable for you.

Are you ready to get started today?

Do you have everything you need to move forward today?

Can we finalize everything we need to move on this today?

Notice the common element between all the closing questions: the word *today*.

We want the client to take notice that today is when they need to take action, not another day. We don't want to ask them if they would like to *think* about it some more. We don't want them to think this offer will be around indefinitely. They need to take action *today*.

If they are not in a position to take action, at this point they will likely tell us they will have to get back to us. That's fine. Find out when they will get back. When can we review again? And book this as another meeting, either by phone or in person.

This is your business. Don't accept flaky responses. You've come this far. It's time to bring it home.

Chapter Seventeen

Closing the Deal

A t this point in time, everything comes down to this moment. This is the moment for which you've worked so hard. It's time to finalize the deal.

There are a lot of sales leaders who will have various forms of closing styles. I really just have two. I don't believe in overcomplicating the process. I've worked hard to get to this point and by the time anyone gets to proposal stage, they should feel more than 80% confident they are going to be getting the deal. That's why the assumptive close is so effective. You and the client are on the same page that you will be moving forward together. If for whatever reason, there's still some uncertainty with the client, you may default to the secondary closing method, which is lovingly named, *the puppy dog close.*"

Regardless, whichever closing technique you decide to use, the client still may come back and ask for more. More of a discount, more of a product, more value, and so on. So it's important to be well-prepared and practiced to know how to address these new challenges so you can get the deal closed quickly and ultimately *Sell More. Faster.*

Assumptive Close

For the most part, I used the Assumptive Close strategy. This assumes that as we go through the sales process we will already be doing business with each other, and that the process of moving through a sales cycle is part of that process.

Language matters a lot. And in the Assumptive Close technique, we use all of our language to act *as if.* We say phrases such as, "when we do business together," as opposed to, "if you decide to do business with us," and, "when we get this implemented," as opposed to, "if you move forward with us."

We are planting the idea in the client's head that they've already chosen us.

Act like their partner from the onset and you'll find your conversation will go much deeper and smoother.

Puppy Dog Close

This is based on the old story of the family who went into the pet shop to look at the puppies. "No, I don't think we're ready," says Mom. "Puppies are a lot of work," says Dad. "Take the puppy home for a night," says the pet shop owner.

"If it doesn't work out, you can always bring him back." No one ever brings the puppy dog back.

The Puppy Dog Close is different than offering a trial or some other type of free offering. See, the family still has to pay for the puppy dog--they just have the option to bring the puppy back.

Now I don't recommend giving away any of your services for free. Nor do I recommend allowing someone to back out of the deal *before* they've had the opportunity to go through part of the service.

People will get buyer's remorse. And if they choose to back out of the deal before they've had the opportunity to experience your service, they never will. Once they say *yes*, and then immediately say *no*, they will almost never go back to *yes*. They made up their mind that the investment was too much, they weren't ready, there was still more to do or whatever other excuse they've convinced themselves was true.

The Puppy Dog Close is more about getting your foot in the door, getting the client to say *yes* to the smallest possible thing first.

Ensure if you do choose to use the Puppy-Dog Close, you are very clear with your client on what the expectations are from their experience. How will they determine if it worked or didn't work for them? And what are the appropriate next steps to take? Directness is your friend in this. If the client is still hesitant to say *yes*, either move them back into the value-creation phase of your sales cycle or choose to cut your losses early. Because nothing is more costly than having and investing in a client who says *yes* and later on says *no*.

Never Negotiate Price

The most common area on which the client will typically push back will be price.

If the client is pushing to try to get a reduced price from you, it usually means one of two things:

They don't understand the full value of the solution presented in front of them, or

They don't have the cash flow to manage the payment solution presented in front of them.

More often than not, a price negotiation can be solved with a payment solution.

What I end up seeing with many entrepreneurs and small business owners who are challenged on the price is them immediately giving the discount because they are afraid of losing the deal.

The deal will not be lost at this point. The client is not going anywhere. You're more than 80% sure you're getting the deal, right? So feel free to play this game. Not all is lost. It's fair to give something up to get something in return.

If you're not more than 80% sure you're getting the deal, see if you can push the client back into the value creation phase. "We're obviously a fair way off in both solution and price. Why don't we go back to the drawing board and ensure you are getting only what you absolutely need at this time."

But perhaps you are in a competitive situation and there are multiple vendors delivering proposals. What do you do then?

Start by separating the solution from the price.

We start by asking several questions:

Price aside, is the solution exactly what you need and how you pictured?

On a scale between 1-10, where price is 1 and the right solution is 10, where do you want to see the solution?

What do you like about the other solutions you've seen?

What do you need to see in order to say *yes*?

As was discussed earlier in the book, questions show a genuine interest in the client's needs. Asking questions in the negotiation phase is just as important. This is not the time to be challenging the client's thoughts or answering with what you think is best. Get the client to first agree on a complete solution and then discuss the price. If you haven't agreed to a solution yet, you are not on the same page as the client and there is still more to uncover.

If the client is answering the questions with you and they are all pointing back to price, my favorite question to ask is,

"If one of your client's asked for a price discount, what would you tell them?"

Typically, the person will say something along the lines of, "We never negotiate on price."

To which I respond, "Great. We share that value."

Understanding and being willing to receive the value for the solution you provide is critical as a premium solution provider. If you are working with someone who does not understand or is not willing to pay for the value you provide, that may be a greater reflection on ensuring you are working with clients who are value-aligned with you earlier on in the sales cycle.

Give and Take Negotiations

It never fails that at some point, a client will ask for more in the deal. Some positions and company roles are built that way. Other clients just love to negotiate. Be prepared for this moment because inevitably, it will happen.

The best time to think about what you would want to ask for in a negotiation is *before* you set foot into the boardroom.

Take time to plan and you will be better prepared and have a greater understanding of what you will be asking for and the value you have associated with that ask.

Ideas we typically provide our students in **KO Sales U** include:

Fewer payments or no payments, for a (slightly) reduced price

Referrals

Written or video testimonials

Case Studies

Cash or electronic funds instead of credit card payments

Future business

Longer delivery timeframes

Providing an additional service instead of a price discount

And so on.

As a premium solutions provider, you will do well setting yourself up before this point to command the premium price, and you will find when it comes time to present your price to your client, you will rarely have to negotiate.

But there will always be times when you will.

Whether that is because the client thinks it's "too much," or they don't have access to enough funds, or they need something delivered soon, ask yourself--are you are more interested in the long-term relationship or the immediate financial compensation?

Knowing what else will add value to your company allows you to create more value when you are in a negotiation with a client and will allow you more flexibility.

Once you've determined what else you will be willing to ask for, it is worth preparing what each item (and I recommend creating a list of more than one) is worth to you and your business.

Just because the client asks for a lower price doesn't mean we have to meet it. It's fine to meet somewhere in the middle, as long as both sides are making concessions throughout the process.

Whatever the case, for the client wanting to get the deal for anything less than the price, time or the full solution, it is wise to be well prepared in a give-and-take negotiation strategy.

Chapter Eighteen

Getting Better at Sales

This book by no means is the complete guide to high-value sales strategy. The average person will read this book in about five hours, which is a far cry from the comprehensiveness you can receive from many day-long, week-long, or in the case of **KO Sales U**, 10-week programs.

This book is meant as a guide for those to use to hone their sales skills and learn that sales, as with any other skills, is something which is to be practiced day after day, if they too want to become better at it.

Sales is about practicing. It's about applying the knowledge you've learned. And most importantly, it's about listening to your prospects and creating a relationship first and foremost.

Making sales isn't up to you, it's up to the client.

Meet your client where they are, not where you want them to be.

There are plenty of suggestions throughout this book, and some of you will read them and think they are ridiculous. I only ask you to try them. You'll be surprised by what a client responds to.

And if you truly want to take your sales up to the next level, send me an email at *Kim@KOAdvantage.com* with the subject line *Sell More. Faster.* I'll be happy to help you put the application behind this education and help you become our newest Sales Knockout!

ABOUT THE AUTHOR

Kim Orlesky is the President of KO Advantage Group. She's listed as LinkedIn's top sales influencers and is continuously named as one of the Top Sales Leaders to Follow. She's Startup Canada's Woman Entrepreneur and Success Magazine's most inspirational blogger. She speaks internationally, including at North America's largest entrepreneurial event, Inbound 2017 & 2018, alongside Michelle Obama, Brené Brown, and Deepak Chopra. In 2014, Kim courageously quit her life to backpack solo around the world. When she returned, she turned her passion for sales into one of North America's fastest-growing sales training programs, KO Sales U.

KO Advantage Group Ltd. is the FASTEST-GROWING sales training company focused on high-value B2B services. Our leading course, KO Sales U, is the most comprehensive course to truly teach you the strategies and processes of selling high-value services to businesses. Developed exclusively for business owners and entrepreneurs, this course dives deep into areas many others leave out.

Not all sales cycles are exactly alike. Not all sales courses are the same.

You wouldn't sit in a classroom for three days to learn how to play a sport, so why would you want to learn your sales process the same way?

Sales application is not the same as education. Sales is about doing. That's why we developed a course which teaches concepts and then immediately provides you with the opportunity to apply it to your own sales cycles.

KO Advantage Group also does amazing team-based training, sales inspirational talks and education for all those wanting to gain a huge advantage over their sales strategy.

Sell More. Faster.

Connect with us online:
https://www.linkedin.com/company/koadvantage/
https://www.facebook.com/KOAdvantage/
https://twitter.com/koadvantage